D0442180

Also by Vladimir Pozner

Parting with Illusions

EYEWITNESS

EYEWITNESS

A Personal Account of the Unraveling of the Soviet Union

Vladimir Pozner

Random House

New York

All rights reserved under International and Pan-American Copyright
Conventions
Published in the United States by Random House, Inc., New York, and
simultaneously in Canada by Random House of Canada Limited, Toronto.

Library of Congress Cataloging-in-Publication Data

Pozner, Vladimir.
    Eyewitness / Vladimir Pozner
        p.   cm.
    ISBN 0-679-41202-6 (cloth)
    1. Soviet Union—History—Attempted coup, 1991. 2. Pozner, Vladimir.
    I. Title.
    DK292.P69   1992
    947.085′4—dc20   91-42235

Manufactured in the United States of America
9 8 7 6 5 4 3 2
First Edition

This book is set in Times Roman and Spectra

This book is dedicated to Katherine, Ekaterina, and Peter— my ultimate support and source of strength.

When tyranny is abroad,
submission is a crime.
　　　　　—*Andrew Elliot, 1756*

Those who expect to reap the
blessings of freedom must, like
men, undergo the fatigue of
supporting it.
　　—*Thomas Paine*
　　　"The American Crisis" 1776

Acknowledgments

Far too many people contributed to the making of this book for me to name even a small number of them. Should I have attempted to do that, I would not have succeeded. For I do not know most of those people. I would not recognize them were I to meet them in the streets of Moscow—as I certainly have.

They are the people who built and manned the barricades around the White House of Russia between August 19 and August 21, 1991.

Without them, this book could not have been written.

Without them, I would probably be in jail.

Without them, the world would now be a very different and very dangerous place. So first and foremost, I wish to acknowledge them.

I also express my gratitude to those without whose help I would have never attempted to write this book:

Ludmila Frolova—for her research.

Fred Hill—for his unflagging support.

Ann Godoff—for not allowing me to give up.

Contents

ACKNOWLEDGMENTS   xi

INTRODUCTION   xv

SUNDAY, AUGUST 25, 1991   3

ALL THE PRESIDENT'S MEN   10

MONDAY, AUGUST 19, 1991   45
Flashback: The Principles of Nina Andreyeva   50
Flashback: Tbilisi, the Dress Rehearsal   82
Flashback: "Companyyyyyy . . . Right!" The Scuttling
    of the "500 Days"   99

TUESDAY, AUGUST 20, 1991   111
Flashback: Shotgun on Red Square   116
Flashback: The Dark Days of December   128
Flashback: Vilnius, the Minicoup   144
Flashback: Here Comes the Military-Industrial
    Complex   157

WEDNESDAY, AUGUST 21, 1991 166
Flashback: Backlash 170
Flashback: A Pavlovian Reflex 176
Flashback: "Boris, You Are Wrong!" 188
Flashback: The Calm Before the Storm 208

THE AFTERMATH 217

Introduction

As a rule, I do not believe in introductions. They usually attempt to tell you what the book is about, which in a way reminds me of the musicologist who, before a concert, takes the stage to tell us what Bach or Chopin *really* wanted to say when they composed this piece.

Let the listener, the viewer, the reader decide. If he or she can't make heads or tails of the work, well, so be it. But what a marvelous thing it is when we are forced to actually *think,* actually engage our minds in a serious effort to understand, instead of relying on someone else's recipe, quickly and conveniently microwaved for our consumption.

So why have I done precisely what I am so strongly against? Because, frankly, I believe there can be exceptions to any rule and feel this is one.

Westerners were given the most extensive blow-by-blow coverage of the August 19 to August 21 Soviet coup and its failure that one could hope for. In that sense the media were brilliant. What Westerners did not get was context, background, a historical framework allowing them to put the coup in proper perspective.

That is what I have attempted to do by introducing a number of "flashbacks" throughout the narrative of what I saw, heard, and felt through those three momentous days. The coup did not just happen—like Topsy. It was the result of complex events which, when they occurred, seemed separate and unrelated. In fact, they were part of a most intricate pattern of forces, each pulling the country in a slightly different direction, but as a whole leading to the same end.

It is my hope that as readers follow the events back and forth in time, they will come away with a better understanding of all those elements that, much like chemicals, were far less powerful when separate than they were in their fusion.

If that hope of mine is realized, I will be able to take satisfaction in the knowledge of having furnished my readers with both an understanding of and a feeling for the forces that were unleashed by Mikhail Gorbachev in 1985 and that, galvanized by the failed coup of August 1991, led to the dissolution of the Soviet Union.

EYEWITNESS

SUNDAY, AUGUST 25, 1991

The white-blue-red flags of Russia snapped smartly in the strong wind blowing off the Moskva River. The biggest flew atop the Russian Federation's government building, a wedding-cake-like structure built during the Brezhnev era. It was a building that, while standing, stood for nothing—a huge memorial to a bureaucracy that produced endless and, for the most part, meaningless papers.

The Russian Soviet Federative Socialist Republic, far and away the largest of the fifteen comprising the Union of Soviet Socialist Republics, was also far and away the least independent. "Independent" is a misleading word for any of the republics since all fifteen were subject to the unquestionable rule of the Central Committee of the Communist Party. But while the fourteen non-Russian republics had the trappings of autonomy—their own Academy of Sciences, their own Communist Party, their own official mission in Moscow—the Russian republic had nothing of the sort.

Russia was, for all practical purposes, perceived by most of the world as being the U.S.S.R. But that perception led to a view that Russia, in one sense, was just about everything and, in another, nothing at all, a land mass spattered here and there with people. So when that preposterous-looking edifice went up on the bank of the Moskva River facing the Ukraina Hotel, it was met with derision and anger by the many Muscovites and Russian visitors to the country's capital. They were people who shared kitchens and bathrooms (or an outhouse) in dilapidated, substandard housing, who for years and years had waited for the day when the endless promises of "an apartment for every Soviet family" would finally come true, who had watched with helpless rage as other, "more equal" members of society, party, and local government functionaries—to say nothing of those who could afford to pay huge bribes—moved into new housing that had been promised to them.

At best, the building had been ignored—people refused to acknowledge its existence. At worst, it was despised and hated. Now everything had changed. Now the White House of Russia, as it had come to be called during the three days of the coup, had become a symbol of the people's struggle for freedom and self-respect. . . .

I stood on the steps leading from the embankment up to the building's main entrance and watched as people walked about, caressing the walls with their eyes, looking with wonder, pride, and love at the young men, many dressed in Afghan war battle fatigues and wearing headbands, who continued to stand guard here on this August Sunday. They were reluctant to leave not only (or even mainly) because of what they might have perceived as a remaining threat to Boris Yeltsin, but because this was their place of glory. This was where they had fought the good fight, this was where they had reasserted their dignity, this, finally, was where many had achieved their summit, their "starlit hour" as they say in Russian. This was the stage upon which they had played out a drama watched by the entire world. Stepping down meant going back to the doldrums of everyday existence. It meant, in a way, disappearing.

I stood and watched, and as I did this, I spoke softly into a tiny tape recorder I cradled in my hand:

"There still are barricades on the steps of the White House that face the river. But they are really more decorative than anything else—stacks of heavy-duty metal wiring, long, iron pipes and rods used to reenforce concrete, splintered boards and large rocks, all piled one upon the other, the metal pipes and rods sticking out in all directions so that some of these structures remind me of a prehistoric porcupine. . . . The stairway is terraced, and right in the middle of the main terrace there stands something that could best be described as a huge painting. On a bright yellow background we see the imperial eagle of tsarist Russia. Its two heads, predatory beaks wide open, red tongues showing, glare right and left. Above the painting, crowning it as it were, Jesus hangs nailed to a cross. . . . A Russian Orthodox priest sits behind a table in front of the painting. Small candles, placed in glass receptacles to protect them from the wind, burn brightly amid the flowers strewn over the table. Two plates, placed on either end of the table, hold money—mainly five- and ten-ruble notes—donated by people to help the families of the three young men who were killed during the coup. . . . A newlywed couple walk up the stairs. They put money into one of the plates and ask the priest to bless them here in front of this makeshift monument to those who saved democracy in Russia. . . .

"As you walk from the White House of Russia toward Tchaikovsky Street and the underpass where three men were killed in the early morning hours of August 20, you see coup-related graffiti: HANG THE JUNTA!, YOUR TIME HAS COME, REDBELLIES!, FUCK THE PRICKS! But as you get closer to the underpass, the tone of the writing changes: REMEMBER AUGUST OF '91!, TREMBLE, COMMIES!.

"As you approach the entrance to the underpass, you see the flowers—thousands of them lying like islands on the asphalt. No transportation, public or otherwise, is being allowed through this part of the Garden Ring today; the entrance to the underpass is still blocked off by three or four trolley cars. I would say that they stand there, except they don't: Their tires are deflated, and so they seem to have sunk down on their haunches, dented and battered, all windows blown out by the ramming fury of the armored cars that tried to crash through them on that fateful night. People come up and touch them, children explore their insides as if they were mysterious vehicles from another civilization. . . .

"Amid the rectangular and oval islands of flowers burn hundreds of candles. There, too, lie half loaves of bread, hard-boiled eggs, pieces of fruit, bottles of wine, pieces of candy wrapped in paper—all these for the souls of those who died right here on the hard asphalt of this underpass. People keep coming and coming; they bring little gifts and souvenirs for the dead. . . . Here, too, the white-blue-red flag of Russia blows in the wind, hangs down from the walls of the underpass. . . . A sailor's hat lies on a bed of flowers, the ribbons spread out so that one can read the inscription: NORTH SEA FLEET. Above that, on the underpass wall in white paint: GORBACHEV IS SHIT! A little farther down along the wall, we see an Orthodox cross and the words GOD HELP US. And then more and more inscriptions: BURY OUR HEROES ON RED SQUARE; ETERNAL MEMORY TO YOU, BOYS; PUT YANAYEV IN FRONT OF A FIRING SQUAD!; CPSU = SS . . .

"Just outside the underpass, on the corner of Protochniy Street and the Garden Ring, several pictures and what seem to be proclamations have been glued to a building wall. On the sidewalk below, candles burn amid flowers and donations. One of the papers on the wall says: THIS PLACE HAS BEEN WASHED WITH THE BLOOD OF A YOUNG MAN

WHO TRIED TO STOP A TANK. BEND YOUR KNEE TO HIM. People approach, read, then bow and place flowers and money on this shrine to one of the martyrs of the coup. Many are dressed in black. Some of them, mostly women, weep. . . ."

The wind had subsided. For the first time in four days, the sun shone down from a perfectly blue sky. In the background, distant loudspeakers carried the voice of Elena Bonner addressing a mass rally at Manezh Square. This was the day of the funeral, when the three victims of the coup were to be buried. . . .

But before the funeral there would be a grand ceremony, which would be attended by as many as a million and a half people. I would be among them, whispering into my tape recorder, looking out over the sea of humanity that strained to see the three caskets, watching two crazed women who had lost their sons in the Afghan war and who now walked like human billboards between two sheets of cardboard covered with pictures of their sons and bearing the inscription: THOSE THREE DIED FOR FREEDOM. WHAT DID MY SON DIE FOR? I would watch as Boris Yeltsin and Stepan Silayev, president and prime minister of Russia, walked purposefully out of Entrance 8 of the White House, surrounded by Kalashnikov-carrying bodyguards. I would watch them approach the three caskets placed between the two walls of humanity in the street running parallel to the building. The two men stood there, heads bowed, silent, somehow both larger than life, then did an about-face and strode briskly back into the building with their silent and fierce protectors around them. And I would wonder why Gorbachev was not there.

That evening when I returned home, I wrote President Gorbachev a letter. I wanted to have it published in a national daily, but never got around to sending it. I'm glad I didn't—in those days when Gorbachev was being dragged facedown through the mud by Yeltsin, it would not have been morally right to do that. But now, after the coup, I would like to unburden myself and let out what I felt then—let it out the way it was then, without the benefit of hindsight provided by the time that has passed:

Dear Mikhail Sergeyevich,
You will probably not be surprised if I tell you that I am happy to see you back. I am glad that you are safe and sound, that neither you, nor any members of your family, were hurt. I express my sincere joy with the hope that you will understand that what I have to say in no way reflects what might be interpreted as anti-Gorbachev bias on my part. I was never anti-Gorbachev. On the contrary, during the entire period of your time in power I was one of your most ardent supporters. Even during the last three years or so, when both in the Soviet Union and abroad, but especially in the former, you were more and more harshly criticized, I was among those who stood by you and defended your policies. I find it necessary to say all this because what follows will hardly please you and, even worse, may make it sound as if I had never been a Gorbachev supporter.

I believe that a leader of any country must have certain qualities. Without them, a person cannot aspire to lead. Among these qualities, one of the most important is the ability to choose the right people, to select those who will work with you. What this probably has to do with is a kind of political intuition, a political sixth sense in determining who really supports your vision and who only pretends to. Without that sixth sense, no political leader can hope to succeed. But that is only the half of it. Without that gift, or quality, no political leader can aspire to play his role as the people's choice.

Allow me to clarify that statement. The people elect their leader on the basis of the political platform, the political program this particular person proposes. If, however, this person, as it turns out, is not capable of achieving what he set out to do, he can justly be accused of having misled the people who elected him to office—and there can be no doubt whatsoever that no goal can be attained if the people appointed to office by that leader are, in fact, not supporters of his program.

I write all this, as it were, to set the context for what I have to say.

Mikhail Sergeyevich, we have just stared down into an abyss. Those people who came to power in the early morning hours of August 19 were not just power hungry, their goal was not only to do away with the policies you had initiated, they were not simply interested in destroying your proclaimed program. We now know that they planned to destroy their political opponents, we now know that they wished to transform the entire country into one huge gulag. This we now know.

These people, Mikhail Sergeyevich, from first to last were selected by none other than yourself. Not only selected, for you stood by them, you recommended them, you supported them—you, Mikhail Sergeyevich, did this. And you must be held responsible for that.

But not only for that.

You, Mikhail Sergeyevich, not only handpicked those people, but you also in fact got rid of those who were your most ardent, most steadfast, most trustworthy and stalwart followers. I have in mind Alexander Yakovlev, Eduard Shevardnadze, Vadim Bakatin, Stanislav Shatalin—in short, those who, much like Bayard of ancient times, were without blemish or reproach where your cause was concerned. You could have and should have put all your faith in them. Instead, you let them go. And in their place you appointed people who then not only betrayed you, but also were people to whom democracy was totally foreign, people who wished to push the country back to its old political boundaries—no matter how much blood would be spilled in the process.

Mikhail Sergeyevich, in light of what has transpired, you no longer have the moral right to lead the country. Where are the guarantees that once again you will not choose to appoint the wrong people? Where are the guarantees that you will not repeat the same mistakes (if, indeed, those were only mistakes on your part and nothing else)? I would like you to understand that if you were a truly responsible person, you would resign. Simultaneously, you would call for universal, direct presidential elections. I do not believe you have the moral fibre to do this. You will do everything you can to hang on, and even if you do call for early elections, I am sure you will run for office. With that in mind, I feel obliged to tell you the following:

Mikhail Sergeyevich, I will vote against you. I will also appeal to one and all to follow my example.

Sincerely,

Vladimir Vladimirovich Pozner

ALL THE PRESIDENT'S MEN

The men who engineered the coup have been presented by the Western media in predictably stereotypical fashion. You have the "faceless party hacks" (Baklanov, Pavlov, Starodubtsev, Tizyakov, Yanayev), and the "evil, brutal, scheming KGB-military alliance" (Kryuchkov, Pugo, Yazov). They have been presented as bumbling, inept, stupid, not even capable of carrying off a coup when they controlled the armed forces, the KGB, the police, and the Party. It has been said that they were not even ruthless enough to spill the blood that would have won the day for them. They have been Hollywood-cast to fit the somewhat gross, repulsive, and yet somehow comical image of what the "commie-Russkie" is supposed to look like, sound like, and be like, from the Soviet ambassador in Stanley Kubrick's classic *Dr. Strangelove: Or How I Learned to Stop Worrying and Love the Bomb,* to the Wendy's hamburger commercial about the Russian fashion show in which women's choices are ludicrously few. And then they have these funny Russian names—another reason why they should really not be considered completely human (although for the life of me I can't understand why, say, Pavlov and Yanayev are funny names, while Bush and Quayle are not).

Difficult as this may prove to be, I will try to present these men as individuals—people with likes and dislikes, some extremely intelligent, others less so, people who were far from inept and, indeed, ready to do whatever was necessary to win. I have met with some of them, interviewed others, and there are a few with whom I have never had any contact. But as a journalist I have followed their careers and I have read just about everything they have ever written or said in public. I submit for your consideration what I have learned about these men and the conclusions I have drawn. I do this with the hope that it will help you understand the complexities of each issue. I also do it with the absolute certainty that, while it may be easier and more comfortable to deal with predigested data—add water, stir, and swallow—the result is very much akin to taking a tranquilizer: It dulls your senses, your intellectual ability to challenge, your natural gift to see more than a unidimensional world.

This is not to say that I consider my interpretation to be definitive. Rather, it is an attempt to look at these people in somewhat broader and more complex terms than "bad guys vs. good guys" and by doing so help the reader acquire a better understanding of the players who engineered and participated in the momentous events which, in effect, ended *perestroika* on August 19, 1991.

Gennadi Yanayev

I met Yanayev on several occasions between 1968, when he was appointed chairman of the U.S.S.R. Committee of Youth Organization (CYO), and 1980, when he became secretary of the All-Union Central Trade Union Council. My first impression of him never changed, and the impression was not a good one. He had come up through the Young Communist League ranks, and that had left an indelible mark on the way he spoke—somewhat gruffly, somewhat coarsely, hinting at a kind of intimacy between himself and you that really never existed, the buddy-buddy-slap-on-the-back-meet-my-pal style, something totally external, something meant to con you, something that translated into an arrogant scorn for your intelligence. He struck me as being vain and pompous as he played the role of senior statesman, now and then patting his clumpy hair he seemed to be so proud of, looking at you from under bushy eyebrows that hung over a meaty nose. His eyes lit up, as I recall, only when the conversation turned to one of two subjects: women and booze.

Vain, pompous, disgusting—yes, but not a fool. No fool made the kind of career this country boy made.

Born in 1937 in the region of Gorky (now Nizhny Novgorod) into a peasant family, he went from high school to the Gorky Agricultural Institute (class of '59), then later went on to receive a degree in law and an M.A. in history.

His first job was that of a mechanic in a rural area not far from Gorky—that was in 1959—after which he was upgraded to engineer. Yanayev soon showed a distinct penchant for work with the Young Communist League (often called the Komsomol), and by 1963 he had risen through the ranks to the post of second secretary of the Gorky Regional Komsomol Committee. Three years later he took over the number one position and did so well that in 1968 he moved to Moscow as chairman of the U.S.S.R. YCL. He headed that organization for twelve years—an amazingly long period, considering how many people desired to have that post, offering as it did almost limitless travel abroad. In 1980 Yanayev moved to the Union of Soviet Friendship Societies as deputy chairman, where he spent six years.

By the time Yanayev received his next posts—secretary

of the Soviet Trade Unions (1986), then deputy chairman (1989), and chairman (1990)—he had acquired a certain degree of respectability. Eighteen years of contacts with endless foreign delegations, as well as foreign travel, had somewhat smoothed the surface, if nothing more. His career accelerated: After only four months as head of the country's entire (and fully corrupt) Trade Union network, he was elected to the Politburo (July 1990) and appointed Central Committee secretary. Five months later, in December, he was nominated by Gorbachev to the post of vice president of the U.S.S.R. and, after a pitched battle in the Parliament, was confirmed.

Of all those intimately involved in the coup, Yanayev was probably the least intelligent and the least dangerous. I feel certain he was selected for leadership by the plotters for two reasons: one was formal, his vice presidential post which made him the constitutional heir to the presidency; the other was his obvious lack of character, which was how he could be controlled. In the final analysis, Yanayev was quite a typical product of the worst the Young Communist League could produce—an obnoxious combination of amorality, immorality, opportunism, and a decided bent for vodka. Rumors have it that on the morning of August 22, when the coup had fallen apart, Yanayev could not be reached in his office or at home. When he was finally found, he was in a drunken stupor—it took several hours before he could even begin to understand what had happened.

Valentin Pavlov

Born in 1937, Valentin Pavlov is a graduate of Moscow's Institute of Finances and Economy; he began his professional career as a finance inspector—the Soviet equivalent of an auditor. He joined the Communist Party in 1962, when he was twenty-five—pretty much par for the course. Those who have known Pavlov over the years characterize him as a man who is well grounded in economic theory, who has strong opinions on that subject and who, generally speaking, gets his way—no matter what it takes. He is also supposed to be a heavy drinker.

Bull-necked and broad shouldered, Pavlov tends to lower his voice and thrust forward his crew-cut head in an argument, thereby increasing his bull-like image. He speaks forcefully and clearly, enunciating words with the precision of a well educated person—which he is. His stride is purposeful, he exudes energy. He seems to carry with him a sign saying, "Don't mess with me."

Pavlov first attracted national attention when he became the U.S.S.R.'s minister of finance in 1989. One of his first steps was to propose a new general tax law—that was in 1990—which was met with universal disapproval by the population.

In January of 1991 Pavlov was nominated by President Gorbachev to the post of prime minister and was confirmed by the U.S.S.R. Supreme Soviet. Almost immediately after that, during a press conference, Pavlov categorically denied rumors concerning forthcoming monetary reform; his deputies did the same in rebutting stories according to which all 100- and 50-ruble bills in circulation would be taken off the market and replaced with new ones. But only a few days after those official denials, all old 100- and 50-ruble bills were declared invalid. The outraged nation demanded an explanation from the prime minister. Without blinking an eyelid, Pavlov picked up on an earlier statement made by KGB chief Vladimir Kryuchkov, but with embellishments:

"A plan to dump a large mass of money on our market has been in the making for a long time. This kind of money dumping can be achieved by different means, one of them being the buying up of large-denomination bank notes. That is precisely what certain Soviet banks as well as several private banks in Austria, Switzerland, and Canada have been doing. . . . These methods are not new, they have been used elsewhere when the goal was to weaken a given political order, get rid of certain political leaders. In our case, someone wants to get rid of our president. . . . It was our duty to thwart those plans to the best of our abilities. As for how well we did—let history be the judge."

Pavlov is one of the players I did not meet personally. But he was one of the chief players and as such one to whom I refer often throughout the book; that, I hope, will help the reader arrive at a somewhat fuller understanding of this man who, by and large, never made a secret of his pros and cons but lied when it served his purpose.

One more point: Pavlov worked diligently to convince the population at large that America and Americans would not come to their rescue and, what's more, there was something shameful about asking to be helped:

". . . I do not believe in it both as a professional and as a normal human being because I know the American system. In America there is no such thing as State finances per se—they have a federal budget determined by Congress. To give money to the Soviet Union, you must go to the Congress and convince the representatives of the American taxpayer that they should furnish the Soviet Union with aid for free, say, because of its pretty blue eyes. Believe me, that is not an easy thing to do, especially considering that you and I will all have to line up behind, say, Israel and Nicaragua. Whoever feels like doing that, go right ahead, but count me out."

Dmitri Yazov

Dmitri Yazov was appointed minister of defense by default. He owes his job to a cocky German kid, Mathias Rust, who flew his little plane solo from Finland, across the Soviet border, over some of the most defense-sensitive areas of the country, and landed in Red Square—all of this without being picked up by the Soviet Union's air defense system. That was a perfect opportunity for Gorbachev to shake up the Soviet High Command, starting with Minister of Defense Sokolov and Air Force Commander Koldunov, and including several others. It had never been easy to fire military brass, even for the general secretary. It would have been doubly difficult for Gorbachev who, by May of 1987, had really begun to show his *perestroika* hand and was upsetting not a few people in the military. Rust was a godsend; he legitimized Gorbachev's decision to retire several top marshals and generals and neutralized any dissatisfaction on the part of the army.

Yazov was a career officer. Born in the little village of Yazov near the Siberian city of Omsk in 1923, he signed up for active duty at age eighteen and went on to fight in World War II from start to finish. He chose a military career and proved to be a capable officer and commander. In 1956 he was graduated from the prestigious Frunze Military Academy; eleven years later he received a degree from the elite Academy of the General Staff of the U.S.S.R. Armed Forces.

In a society where nationality, class origin, politics, and profession were key career factors, Yazov was a personnel department chief's dream come true: Russian by nationality, peasant by birth, a World War II veteran, a Party member—his bio was perfect. In January of 1987 he was promoted to deputy minister of defense, and only five months later the Rust caper catapulted him to the top defense job.

Yazov was nobody's fool. The tough, gruff facade hid a keen intelligence. I remember calling him up with the intention of inviting him to participate in a TV show I was planning to do about the Soviet armed forces, their place in society, and how people felt about them. It was a funny conversation:

"Dmitri Timofeyevich?"

"Yes."

"Hello. This is Vladimir Vladimirovich Pozner."

"Well, well, well . . . And what can I do for you?"

The sarcastic tone of voice, the choice of words—neither left any doubts whatsoever as to how Marshal Yazov felt about me.

"I am going to be doing a show on the armed forces and society. I don't have to tell you what a controversial subject that is, and I was hoping you would agree to be my guest."

"You hoped wrong. I have a job to do. You pesky journalists want my face to be all over television. What do you think I am, an actor?"

"No, Dmitri Timofeyevich, I know you are not an actor—at least in the conventional sense. And if you don't want to do the show or contribute to it, well, that's just too bad. I'll have to do it the best I can—and don't blame me when I tell people the minister of defense refused to help."

"Ha, you journalists love to twist words, don't you. Did I say I would not help you? Did I? I said I couldn't participate. I will see to it that you get all the help you need. Does that sound right?"

"Yes, I thank you very much."

What that conversation shows is Yazov's attitude toward the democratic media—although I must admit he sent me three generals to participate in the show. Yazov did not like democrats, period—not just the democratic media. He was once heard to state:

"I personally fail to understand who are the democrats and who are the conservatives. Those who defend the socialist view, those who are for preserving our Union, they are considered conservative. Those who are ready to tear the country apart, who want everyone to lock themselves up in their little nationalist apartments, who want to break up the army—these people are called democrats."

Neither did Yazov have much tolerance for the Russian Parliament. Addressing a group of military men, all deputies to the U.S.S.R. Supreme Soviet, he said:

"I thank you all for having faced down the government of Russia. . . . We have been so victimized by the Tbilisi syndrome,* that we have crawled back into our dens. We all hate the notion of private property, and that unites us. We are true patriots; we must act as one!"

Yazov openly supported the idea of military participation in formulating policy—and said as much during an interview with the progressive *Moskovskiye Novosty* weekly, when he was asked whether the armed forces had any intention of interfering in the political process.

So what kind of a man was Dmitri Yazov? A blunt, brutal, cunning, power-hungry general? It would be nice if he fitted that image, but . . .

Differing from all the other military brass, Yazov did not have and never had a *dacha*—a luxurious country estate, one of the privileges of the Soviet elite. He lived a spartan life. He dreamed of the day when he could retire. As his wife Emma said in a postcoup interview with the *Komsomolskaya Pravda* daily after her husband's arrest, "He was planning to retire, we often spoke about that. We are not wealthy people, we have no *dacha* of our own, we don't even own a car. . . . He was always honest in what he said and did, he cared deeply about what was happening to his country. . . . I love him and will always love him."

---

* Yazov was referring to the events that occurred in Tbilisi in April of 1989; they are discussed in this book.

Vladimir Kryuchkov

Short, with a fringe of white hair around his balding pate, Kryuchkov has mild blue eyes which look out at you with vague curiosity through thick glasses. His face is nondescript, neither attractive, nor repulsive. Nothing stands out, nothing catches the eye. The perfect face for a spy.

I met Kryuchkov only once, when I asked him to tape an on-camera interview for my show, *An Evening with Vladimir Pozner*, in Moscow. That was in December of 1990, a time when *perestroika*'s supporters seemed to be on the run, a time when the hard-liners had "come out of the trenches" (an expression coined by Gorbachev). Kryuchkov had made a television appearance that same month on the evening news, an appearance that had rocked the country. Now I wanted to get his end-of-year forecast.

Kryuchkov took my call and, after hearing me out, agreed to do not an interview but a statement. He would write it himself, he said, and read it. I agreed, not really having much of a choice, and was in his office on the fourth floor of KGB headquarters on Kuznetsky Most Street two days before the show. This was my first time in the KGB chairman's office. I don't know what I expected to see, but what I actually saw was a large, though not gigantic, oak-paneled room, tastefully furnished with a conference table off to the left and a desk at the far end. On the wall behind and above the desk hung a portrait of Mikhail Gorbachev.

In a way, the office was as impersonal as the man who worked there. His handshake was firm and dry, his greeting courteous. He sat down at his desk and read his statement. "How was it?" he asked, once he had finished. I told him he had been a little bit stiff. "Shall I read it over?" he asked. I said I would appreciate it. And he read it over. "Is it good now?" he wanted to know. I said it was, realizing it would not get any better, even if he read his statement twenty times. The problem was both with Kryuchkov and with what he was saying: Both were bland and, with the exception of his "best wishes to the Soviet people in the coming New Year," completely impersonal. He thanked me for having offered him this chance to speak on television. I thanked him for having taken the time to speak to me. We shook hands—and that was it. And if anything surprised me about this meeting, it was the unsurprising character of the man I had met. And yet, he was the product par excellence of his time.

Vladimir Kryuchkov was born into a working class family in 1924. He went to work during World War II, when he was in his teens, in one of Stalingrad's (now Volgograd) defense plants. He was active in the Young Communist League and soon became secretary of one of the League's regional committees. By then he had moved to another city on the Volga, Saratov, where he enrolled in the Saratov Juridical Institute. From 1946 to 1947 he worked as a prosecutor in the district attorney's office. In 1947 he was appointed chief prosecutor, a post he held until 1951.

Having obviously made a name for himself, Kryuchkov was selected for further grooming and sent to Moscow's Higher School of Diplomacy, an academic institution specifically created to train personnel for the Soviet Union's foreign service. Selection was based on several factors, not the least of which were Communist Party membership (Kryuchkov joined the Party at age twenty in 1944), class origin (preference was given to working class people), and nationality (Russians first, Jews last). Over the years, I had the opportunity to lecture at this somewhat unusual educational institution where, as I soon learned, most of the "students" were former Party workers who had to be taught at least one foreign language and etiquette—things like how to hold a knife and fork.

The students were, on the whole, a grim and very conservative bunch. Most of them were brought in from the "great heartland," that is, from places far from Moscow, Leningrad, or any of the real intellectual, and therefore more cosmopolitan, communities. Usually they were people with narrow views, people who swore by the Party, who saw this opportunity not only as a godsend, but as a Party reward for their loyalty. I spoke only twice there, for my views were far too liberal. It was not only the dean who decided against having me speak there again but also many of the students; several, as I was told, had written letters of protest to the dean's office. Others—this was confidential information—had reported me to the KGB for spreading "subversive thoughts." That is the institution the up-and-coming Vladimir Kryuchkov attended for two years.

Upon graduating in 1955, Kryuchkov was sent to Hungary, where he served in the Soviet embassy as third secretary. The ambassador was none other than Yuri Andropov, the future chairman of the KGB and future general secretary of the Communist Party of the Soviet Union. During the days of the bloody Hungarian uprising of 1956, crushed by overwhelming Soviet military force, Kryuchkov must have worked in very close contact with Andropov, a situation that was to play a most important role in his future.

Kryuchkov returned to Moscow in 1959, where his career took a quantum leap: He landed a job as a staff member of the Central Committee. There is plenty of reason to believe his patron in this matter was Andropov, who in those days was a senior official of the Central Committee. Kryuchkov did well, moving from the position of researcher to head of sector and finally to the influential post of Central Committee secretary aid.

In 1967 Kryuchkov was offered a position with the KGB, where by that time Andropov had been appointed chairman. Kryuchkov moved up the ranks, finally reaching the tremendously powerful position of head of the First Department—the one responsible for espionage.

In 1988 Mikhail Gorbachev personally appointed Vladimir Kryuchkov chairman of the KGB. From that point on, he became a very visible person on the Soviet political horizon.

His name appears often in this book, as do those of most of the plotters (the exceptions being Baklanov, Tizyakov and, to a lesser degree, Starodubtsev). The reader will have ample opportunity to draw his or her own conclusions concerning the role Kryuchkov played in the years leading up to the coup, as well as in the coup itself. Nevertheless, I would like to impress on the reader just one preliminary thought: When Kryuchkov was arrested after the coup, he was interviewed by a colleague of mine, Vladimir Molchanov, who asked him whether or not he regretted anything he had done. Kryuchkov's answer was unequivocal: No, he did not. He had done nothing to be ashamed of, nothing that, in his opinion, could have hurt the Motherland.

Those were not empty words, Kryuchkov was not posing. He spoke what he believed—and he believed what he had been taught from the days of the Battle of Stalingrad through the years in the Academy of Foreign Relations to the years of work with his mentor, Yuri Andropov.

Vladimir Kryuchkov could not but have been a driving force (if not the intellect) behind the coup.

Boris Pugo

The first organization in the Soviet Union to have an official public relations office was . . . the KGB. That must have occurred in 1989 or 1990. I do not know which organization became the second or third, but my guess is that the Ministry of the Interior, usually referred to in Russian as the MVD, must have been not far behind. Being as openly critical as I was of the government and especially of the hard-liners, I could not have been more surprised when I received a phone call from an MVD colonel informing me of the gala opening of the MVD's public relations office. Would I accept an invitation? Overcoming my surprise, I quickly accepted. The colonel gave me the date, the time, and the place, then followed up a few days later with an official invitation.

I do not remember the day or even the month, but I think it was in June of 1991. On that day I had been delayed, so instead of arriving at 3 P.M. I got there at half past three. Again, to my surprise, there were several police officers standing on the sidewalk waiting for me. They allowed me to park in a No Parking area, and accompanied me into the building. I was quickly seated in the front row of a room where at least three hundred people had assembled. There were photographers and TV cameras everywhere.

I hardly had the time to take stock of the situation before I was called upon to say a few words about the occasion. TV lights went on and flashes went off as I took the floor, still wondering what this was all about. I recall saying something about how surprised I was to be invited, considering my status as an independent journalist who was on nobody's payroll. I said I hoped this was a sign that the MVD was changing and would be more open to journalists than it had been in the past.

As I said that, I suddenly noticed the minister of the MVD, Boris Pugo. Due to my hurried entrance I had not spotted him, but now I saw him watching me with a little smile on his face. Pugo had always reminded me of some sad-sack character out of French Grand Guignol. He had the face of a rubber doll—you felt you could push it in on one side and the other side would balloon out. The middle part of his head was completely bald, but on the left and right he had these tufts of hair that tended to stand on end in the most comical way.

After the press conference Pugo came up to me, shook my hand, and told me how glad he was to see me. "Even though you journalists just can't keep from being nasty, can you?" he said with a smile that somehow looked just a little bit like a sneer. His voice was soft as was his hand, almost pudgy in fact, and his face, now that I was seeing it just a few inches from my own, looked much harder than I had thought. I asked him whether he would be willing to be a guest on my show and to discuss the crime situation in the country. "Any time," he answered. "We officials are always at your service"—the accompanying smile decidedly reminded me more and more of a sneer.

I still don't know why I was invited and given VIP treatment. There must have been a reason—as I later learned, Pugo had personally requested that I be sent an invitation. Had I spent more time with him, I would have asked why. Before leaving I got him to agree to be on my show in September. But the coup happened in August . . .

Boris Pugo was born of Latvian parents in the city of Kalinin, in Russia, in 1937. I suspect his father had been a "Red Latvian" or even, perhaps, a member of the Latvian Sharpshooters, a revolutionary military unit that was one of the Bolsheviks' crack forces; during and after the civil war, the Latvian Sharpshooters were chosen to serve as Lenin's personal bodyguards. Their revolutionary zeal often manifested itself in a total disregard for personal life and limb—as well as for that of the class enemy. When Latvia's Soviet government, briefly established in 1918, was overthrown that same year and the country declared its independence, most of the Red Latvians remained in Russia. In Latvia, where the Communist Party was outlawed and forced underground, they would have been apprehended and incarcerated.

The Hitler-Stalin Pact with its secret protocols changed all that. Latvia was incorporated into the Soviet Union "on popular demand" in 1940 and many of those who had fled in 1918 or who had not returned now did. Pugo's family may have been among them. They may also have returned only after the Soviet army liberated Latvia from German occupation in 1944.

Be that as it may, Boris Pugo got his schooling in the capital city of Riga, where he was graduated at the Riga Polytechnic Institute. That same year he went to work as an engineer at Riga's Electric Machine-Building Plant. However, his professional career was brief: In 1961 Pugo became Young Communist League secretary of the plant's Komsomol Committee—a full-time job with a salary. He joined the Communist Party in 1963 and his Komsomol/Party career blossomed: second secretary, then first secretary of the Proletarian Regional Komsomol Committee, followed by a stint in the Central Committee of the Latvian Komsomol, and from there to the Communist Party post of head of department of Riga's City Committee, then back to Komsomol activity as the top executive for the republic—first secretary of the Central Committee of the Latvian Young Communist League. The next move was to Moscow, where he served as one of the secretaries of the Young Communist League's Central Committee and then moved to the Communist Party's Central Committee with the rank of inspector.

Moscow was a stopover, a grooming place. Pugo returned to Riga, serving first as a staff member of the local Communist Party's Central Committee and then as first secretary of the Riga City Party Committee.

In 1976 Pugo was rewarded with a post in the Latvian republic's KGB; he became its chairman in 1980. Four years later Boris Pugo reached the pinnacle of local power as first secretary of the Latvian Communist Party's

Central Committee. But soon after Mikhail Gorbachev became general secretary in March 1985, things began to change. By 1987 reform was making itself felt. The movement was picking up speed, especially in the Baltics. And so, much like his father before him, Pugo was forced to leave Riga—and left it, as it turned out, forever.

There may have been more than politics and ideology to Soviet Minister of the Interior Pugo's attitude toward recalcitrant republics—that is, republics bent on achieving independence—especially in what concerns the Baltic states. Where the army had its Red Berets, an elite shock force known as the *Spetsnaz* (from the Russian *spetsial'noye naznacheniye:* "special mission"), the Ministry of the Interior had its Black Berets—the OMON (*Otryad Militsii Osobovo Nasnacheniya:* "Special Mission Militia Platoon"). Pugo used the OMON with excessive cruelty in Lithuania, in Latvia, in Armenia, and in Azerbaijan. Was he simply carrying out orders, or was he, in addition to orders, punishing the republics for a past involving his parents and his childhood? I would have loved to interview him on that subject, but that was not to be: Boris Pugo committed suicide as the police were coming to arrest him for his participation in the coup. But that was much later.

Summoned to Moscow from a more and more rebellious Riga in 1987, Pugo was soon elected chairman of the Communist Party's Control Commission—that occurred at the September 1988 Party plenum. Exactly one year later, at another Party plenum, he was elected candidate-member of the Politburo.

A Latvian journalist who knew Pugo since his childhood once commented: "Pugo's greatest gift is his ability to second-guess what the boss wants and then to come up with the political justification for that desire."

That may well have been the reason for Pugo's downfall. But when the end came, Pugo demonstrated the same quiet decisiveness he had always been known for. After having received a phone call from the head of Russia's KGB and being informed they were coming to arrest him, Pugo went into his bedroom, wrote a note to his wife and children asking their forgiveness, lay down on the bed and shot himself in the mouth. Hearing the shot, his wife ran into the room and saw him lying there, blood trickling down his face. She sat down next to his still-warm body, wrote a note to her children, telling them she could not live without the man she loved—and shot herself twice.

Oleg Baklanov

Born in Kharkov, the Ukraine's second-largest industrial center, in 1932, Baklanov started his professional career as a blue-collar worker in the electric engineering industry at age eighteen. Three years later he joined the Communist Party. After taking engineering-by-correspondence courses, he received a degree in 1958 and followed up with an M.A. thesis. Baklanov's determination and intelligence contributed to his rapid rise in industrial management and led to his appointment as general director of one of the country's major industrial defense complexes. In 1976 he was made a deputy minister of something euphemistically called the Ministry of Middle Machine-Building—really the heart of the Soviet defense industry (including missiles, nuclear weapons, etc.), and by 1983 he had moved into the top position of minister.

In 1986 he was elected to the Central Committee. Two years later Baklanov was entrusted with the crucial job of Central Committee secretary responsible for the entire Soviet military-industrial complex. He left that position in April of 1991 to become first deputy chairman of the U.S.S.R. Defense Council—a post he occupied until the failure of the coup.

Baklanov was a People's Deputy, winning a seat as

one of the one hundred "candidates" selected by the Party to "run" on the Communist Party ticket to the national Parliament. He was the recipient, over the years, of such top awards as the Lenin Prize and of such decorations as Hero of Socialist Labor, the Order of Lenin, the October Revolution Order, the Red Banner Order, and several others.

I never met Baklanov, a man who was not in the public eye. I have, however, spoken to people who knew him well and who characterize him as strong, stubborn, and intelligent. Baklanov headed that which, in the final analysis, gave the Soviet Union its superpower status: the production, as well as the research and development, of military weapons. This was also an area that was run like a military establishment. There was never a question of not being able to get whatever budgetary allocations might be called for; the magic words "national security" opened the vaults to the nation's wealth. For a man like Baklanov the idea of having to ask Parliament for funds was as repulsive as it seemed absurd.

One should also not forget that the Soviet planned economy, often called a command economy, had not always been a failure. It had, in fact, been spectacularly successful. The first Five-Year Plans, beginning in 1929, had startled the world in how quickly they had catapulted the Soviet Union into the front ranks of the industrial powers. Much cruelty had been involved, including the labor of political prisoners in the gulag, but the combination of popular support and enthusiasm for the system and an economy totally controlled by the government did, at first, yield amazing results.

Baklanov believed in that kind of setup. He believed in the necessity of giving the military-industrial complex a free hand. He most decidedly did not believe in democratic methods of production, nor in an economic system based on the laws of supply and demand.

I think it is also fair to say that Baklanov believed in the Communist Party and Communism. And even when faith in the idea and the organization which supposedly embodied it seemed to be dying, Oleg Baklanov had an argument which, though perhaps not convincing to everyone, is certainly worthy of consideration:

"Let me make the following comparison. The tragedy and the pathos of Jesus Christ is in that he was not understood by his contemporaries. Yet to this day his ideas live on. A similar thing is now happening with the Communist movement. A large part of the consumer society has repudiated its ideas; many predict the movement's failure, are quick to announce its demise. But in reality, as I see it, that is a serious mistake, a lack of understanding of the process. It is no secret that capitalism incorporated much of Communism's positive and good aspects. And that has been beneficial for all of humankind. That should be highly valued. The wonderful idea of building a Communist society will eventually fire the minds of millions and millions of people. I firmly believe that."

A man of the people who made his way up from blue-collar worker to fill one of the most important and powerful positions in the Soviet, a man who firmly believed he had been able to do this because of the Soviet system of government and the Communist Party, Baklanov remained loyal to his principles and stood as a formidable opponent to those who desired to undo what nearly seventy-four years of Soviet socialism had done.

Oleg Baklanov represented the military-industrial complex. This stern, unsmiling man's signature was on every one of the junta's declarations and decrees. He was, without the slightest doubt, one of the major players.

Vassily Starodubtsev

What most people will remember about Vassily Starodubtsev was what a fool he made of himself during the junta's first and only news conference, held on August 19. When *Izvestia* pundit Alexander Bovin asked him, "How did *you* ever get involved with that company?" Starodubtsev answered with a shrug, "They invited me, so I came."

His is a strange case. Born in a Russian village in 1931, this man of peasant stock worked hard to get a higher education in the field of agriculture, never wavering from his stated goal of helping the *muzhik,* the Russian peasant, have a better life and work more productively. In 1963 he was elected chairman of a collective farm in the village of Novomoskovskoye, not far from the old Russian town of Tula, and immediately began to reorganize it along what he called modern production lines. Starodubtsev was one of the first collective farm chairmen not only to speak out in favor of approaching farming as an agro-industrial business, but to actually implement that view. Since change is always suspect in the Soviet Union, Starodubtsev was soon targeted by local Party and other officials who saw his innovations as a threat.

In those days—the late sixties and mid seventies—journalists supported this champion of new agricultural methods, even though they had to be very careful not to antagonize the Party. But when the collective farm he headed, once one of the poorest and least productive, suddenly began to outproduce just about all other farms in the region, when it doubled, then tripled, then finally quadrupled its output, when it not only paid off its debts but became a real money earner, things changed for Starodubtsev. In 1976 he was awarded the highest decoration of Hero of Socialist Labor, and in 1979 won a State Prize.

The Novomoskovskoye collective farm became a model for others; it was also used to demonstrate the achievements of socialist agriculture.

With the onset of *perestroika,* Starodubtsev's name became associated with progress and reform in agriculture. "Stop telling us what to do, just leave us alone and let us do the job"—that was his motto as he battled Party and government bureaucrats whose job it had traditionally been to oversee Soviet agriculture. Starodubtsev was against outside control of agriculture and in that aspect he was decidedly supportive of the farmers' interests. But what most of us failed to realize, at least initially, was that Vassily Starodubtsev was for control—control of the collective farm by its chairman, the "father" who knew what was best for his "children." Because of that, he could not support the idea of private farms and farmers, for they would be impossible to control.

The argument about what type of agricultural process is the most productive is really an ideological argument, not an economic one. The forced collectivization of the Soviet Union by Stalin in 1929 had much more to do with destroying the so-called *kulak* class, that is to say, the wealthy farmers who had appeared after the revolution, than with any desire to increase agricultural productivity. These men had started out like everybody else: They had been given a plot of land the size of which was based on the number of people in the family. Thanks to hard work, they had prospered. They had become, as Stalin saw it, a bourgeois force in Soviet society, a threat to his power—and he destroyed them.

Ever since that time the U.S.S.R. has suffered the consequences. With the most qualified, most hardworking farmers gone, with collective farm chairmen appointed by Party committees, who were often factory workers sent down to the rural areas to "keep the *muzhiks*" in line, agricultural production began to fall—and that has never changed.

Forced collectivization once again illustrated the ultimate futility of attempts to impose on a person or on people something they do not accept. Forced to work together, farmers demonstrated little zeal. But working the private plots they were given as collective farm members, plots which amounted to about 3 percent of all the cultivated land in the country, they delivered 30 percent of the nation's agricultural produce.

The latter figure does not, however, in my opinion simply support the idea that private ownership of the land is "better" than collective. What is undeniably better is that people should be able to enjoy whatever form of ownership they prefer. If a group of individuals wishes to create a collective farm and own the land, the livestock, and the machinery collectively and collectively share the profits of their labor, so be it. Conversely, individual farming should also be allowed. Time will show which of the two works better. (I instinctively feel the former should—a team is always more productive than an individual, provided the team is made up of individuals who chose to be a team.) In the United States a huge agro-industry is in the process of wiping out the individual farmer who cannot compete with the giants (even though the quality and the taste of his produce is far superior).

With *perestroika* came the idea of privatization, and as the idea grew, as more and more people began to support it, as the first private farmers appeared, Starodubtsev's became a more and more strident voice against progress:

"Those whose aim is to destroy the collective farm system see this as a way to gain political power. They know of the chaos that will follow, that in the first year alone the production of food will drop by half, if not more. After that it is easy to overthrow any government, to take over the seat of power, to pick up a whip and flail away at the peasant—as we did for so many years. What kind of democracy will be left after that? For those people democracy is just a means for achieving a certain end. . . .

"Today's farmer is a different man from the one who

existed seventy years ago; he does not understand what market he is being called upon to be part of. Is it the market he was taught to hate and fear for seventy years? Mind you, several generations have grown up since then, and that hatred has become, shall we say, hereditary. Today's peasant does not as yet understand the market. He is being dragged there—to the market, market, market. . . . What kind of market, I ask you? . . .

"I am categorically against the sale of land and I am certain the majority of peasants share my view. . . . The farmer, what's more, doesn't have the money to buy land. The only ones who can do that are crooks from the shadow economy, and they will do it by proxy, and, once that happens, they will use the land as they see fit to accumulate gigantic personal wealth."

There is really nothing surprising in the junta's having invited this peasant commissar to join their ranks. He shared their politics, he came from the same past; he was dead set against the kind of future Gorbachev was calling the nation to work for.

Alexander Tizyakov

He could be called the mystery man. The first time most of us heard of him was when he participated in the now notorious news conference of August 19. But he was very well known indeed to those whose chief professional activities related to the Soviet defense industries.

Born in 1926, a veteran of World War II, Alexander Tizyakov was demobilized in 1950 and started out in life as a driver. Having no intention of doing that for the rest of his life, he took advantage of his war vet status and enrolled at the Urals Polytechnic Institute in his hometown of Sverdlovsk (now Yekaterinburg, as it was called before the revolution). By 1956 he was working as a technology expert in one of Sverdlovsk's many defense factories. He did some Party work and was elected secretary of his plant's Party committee, but then went back to being strictly professional. He was promoted to chief engineer and, finally, general director.

Tizyakov must have been respected by his peers, as they elected him president of the Association of U.S.S.R. Industrial, Construction, Transportation, and Communications State Enterprises and Conglomerates. He was clearly proud of that post and was known to have made the point that his Association represented virtually the entire country's managerial corps. This, however, was not true. The Association, presided over by Tizyakov, consisted almost exclusively of the military-industrial complex.

On December 6 and 7 of 1990, at a nationwide conference of the Association, Tizyakov made the keynote speech in which he challenged President Gorbachev and stated in no uncertain terms that if legislation was not passed prohibiting strikes, if the former ministerial structure of management was not preserved, if efforts to restructure the country's basic industries was not dropped, there would be hell to pay.

Gorbachev was present at the speech, and even though the proceedings were held behind closed doors, we know what his reaction was: "Are you trying to scare me? Forget it."

Gorbachev's refusal to accept Tizyakov's ultimatum, to bow to the pressure of the military-industrial complex, are what probably led the latter to participate in the coup. According to people who knew Tizyakov over the years and worked with him, like the party secretary of the Sverdlovsk City Committee, Vladimir Denisenko, Tizyakov was always considered a "hard-line Bolshevik"; tough, demanding, direct, he was of the opinion that the post-*perestroika* period would see the restoration of the Communist Party's supremacy. Unconfirmed rumors have it that, had the coup succeeded, Alexander Tizyakov would have been appointed prime minister.

These are the eight men who led the coup. With the exception of Valentin Pavlov, they all came from blue-collar or peasant families, they were all self-made men, and they all owed everything they had achieved to the Soviet system of government. Should we be surprised at their resistance to the radical change brought about by Gorbachev's *perestroika*? At their refusal to allow the Union of republics to break up? At their support of the Party? I don't believe we should.

Much as the picture of a group of blundering boobs or evil plotters might reassure us by reaffirming the stereotypes we have been induced to believe, that image has little to do with reality—as little as an outline sketch of a future portrait has to do with the model.

Although only eight men officially made up the committee that took power on August 19, 1991, there are two more whose roles were so important throughout the period leading up to the coup and during the coup itself that it would be a mistake on my part not to draw the reader's attention to them. This is true especially considering how close both these men were to President Gorbachev: According to trustworthy information, they were the only ones who could call the president directly without going through a secretary, and the only ones who could enter his office without a preliminary appointment.

Valery Boldin
Anyone looking for a photograph of any remotely well-known Soviet person is advised to go to Tass, the official Soviet news agency. Its photo archives are unrivaled insofar as Soviet subject matter is concerned. And yet, when Valery Boldin was arrested for his participation in

the coup and several newspapers applied for pictures, Tass came up with only one very official passport-type looking photo, nothing more. That was remarkable, considering who Boldin was, what kind of power he had, how long he had been close to the very top echelon. It bespoke a truly singular quality, for here was a man whose appetite for power was insatiable, but yet who made a point of keeping a low profile, staying out of the range of any reporter's camera, seeing to it that no one would ever suspect him of desiring to rise any higher—a suspicion fraught with the danger of his career being abruptly terminated.

Boldin was born in 1935. He was an average student, and after graduating from high school in 1953 took a blue-collar job on the Moscow-Ryazan Railroad. A few years later, taking advantage of his "working class experience" (Soviet law allowed high school graduates with a minimum of two years of work experience to enroll in any university without taking competitive entrance exams), Boldin became a student of the Timiryazev Agricultural Academy, majoring in economy. In 1960 he joined the Communist Party and in 1961 he landed a job with the country's most influential newspaper, *Pravda.*

Boldin spent one year at *Pravda* and then, much to everyone's amazement, was picked by Leonid Ilyichev, a secretary of the Communist Party's Central Committee, to be his aide. Why Boldin, many wondered? Later, Ilyichev explained that he had been looking for someone young—Boldin was only twenty-five—whose mind was pliable. Ilyichev was one of the Party's leading ideologues; he was also one of the most well versed in the intricacies of the bureaucratic structure. He set out to teach Boldin the tricks of his trade, and Boldin turned out to be a talented pupil.

Everything seemed peaceful on the horizon, promising Boldin a rosy future, when disaster struck: Khrushchev was ousted from office in October of 1964, Ilyichev was forced to retire, and Boldin was thrown out of the Central Committee. But he was a survivor. Pulling the strings of his Central Committee connections, he enrolled at the Academy of Social Science, an educational institution run by the Communist Party and created for the purpose of producing its top cadres. When Boldin was graduated with honors in 1969, he returned to *Pravda*—this time as the deputy editor of the paper's powerful agricultural department. (What the reader should understand is that any article published in *Pravda* was regarded as being gospel, a journalistic expression of the Party's will; if a *Pravda* article criticized someone or something related to agriculture, that person or thing was finished. On the other hand, a laudatory piece meant nationwide recognition. The chiefs of departments had, therefore, tremendous power. They were courted, wined and dined, and if possible bribed, for they often held the key to people's fates.)

Over the next few years Boldin worked on a thesis concerning the modernization of agriculture in Great Britain; he received his Ph.D. and acquired additional stature. When the old head of the paper's agriculture department retired, Boldin took his place and held it until 1981, when he once again was offered a job as aide to a Central Committee secretary. That particular secretary was responsible for overseeing the state of Soviet agriculture. His name was . . . Mikhail Sergeyevich Gorbachev.

Ilyichev told us why he had picked the young and inexperienced Boldin. Gorbachev has said nothing to explain his choice; however, the reasons are obvious enough. Boldin must have traveled to the country's most important agricultural areas in his capacity as *Pravda* correspondent and later as chief of department. One of those areas was the Stavropol region, where Gorbachev was Party secretary. The two could not but have known each other. Boldin surely must have recognized Gorbachev's up-and-coming status. What's more, under Gorbachev the Stavropol harvests were among the highest in the country and thus were singled out for praise in *Pravda.* The new Central Committee secretary responsible for agriculture could not have found a better aide—a young man who had proven his loyalty, who knew agriculture inside out, including foreign practice, and who, finally, even had Central Committee experience.

Thus Boldin became one of Gorbachev's most trusted people. As Gorbachev rose in the ranks, so did Boldin: in 1985 Boldin became aide to the general secretary of the Communist Party's Central Committee. Two years later he moved one step higher—he was appointed head of something called the General Department. Created by Brezhnev for his chief of staff, Chernenko, this was the Party's nerve center, where all personnel decisions were ultimately made and through which all information passed. The man who headed the General Department could influence the general secretary's most important decisions, for the latter depended on this person's input.

When Mikhail Gorbachev was elected president of the U.S.S.R. in 1989, Valery Boldin became, first, a member of the Presidential Council and finally was appointed presidential chief of staff.

That position gave him almost unlimited power. Anyone who wanted to talk to the president had to go through Boldin; all documents and papers could not reach the president's desk before being scrutinized and vetted by Boldin. There is reason to suspect that Gorbachev's swing to the right, his tendency to turn a deaf ear to the liberals was, at least in part, the result of the distorted information passed on to him by Boldin.

Of the many political alliances in the Soviet Parliament whose members attempted to secure appointments with the president, only the hard-line conservative Soyuz group enjoyed that privilege—thanks to Boldin.

As head of the Central Committee's General Department and, later, presidential chief of staff, Boldin held the keys to Party and State archives; he decided who could and who could not have access to them. For instance, Valentin Falin, the former Soviet ambassador to the Federal Republic of Germany, who under Gorbachev became a secretary of the Central Committee, was given the job of looking into the Party archives for documents relating to the Stalin-Hitler Pact of 1939 and the tragedy of the Katyn forest massacre. Boldin barred him from entry— and there was very little that Falin could do about it.

Totally trusted by Gorbachev, feared and hated by most others, Valery Boldin never allowed himself to be caught in the limelight, preferring to hide in the shadow of his protector—until, that is, he decided that the time had come to betray his patron and make the move that would finally rectify the discrepancy between his very real power and almost total anonymity.

Anatoly Lukyanov

"Anatoly I. Lukyanov was his nondescript, nearly bashful self today as he was summoned into the national limelight by sharp-tongued critics demanding he explain his career role as Mikhail S. Gorbachev's indispensable cipher. . . . 'Strange things started happening in our ideology,' Mr. Medvedev* declared, pleased that Mr. Lukyanov's strength as the methodical factotum and alter ego at the side of Mr. Gorbachev for the past 35 years was being formally institutionalized."

The quote comes from a *New York Times* article published on May 30, 1989, and written by Francis X. Clines of that paper's Moscow bureau. In my opinion Mr. Clines is one of the finest American reporters, a man who com-

---

* Roy Medvedev, considered to be one of the more liberal, pro-*perestroika* People's Deputies.

bines knowledge with style. I quote him to bring up a very important point, namely, how misleading Anatoly Lukyanov's public demeanor was, how he completely fooled even the most intelligent and experienced journalists, including Mr. Clines.

Lukyanov was anything but nondescript. He was decidedly not bashful. His relationship with Gorbachev did date back to the days when they were both students at Moscow University's Juridical Faculty, but factotum and alter ego he was not.

I first met Anatoly Lukyanov when Boris Yeltsin, who had promised to be on my show on December 30, 1990, skipped out at the last minute. With less than two days to go before air time, I had no show. I knew I was not going to get Gorbachev and I decidedly did not want Vice President Yanayev. The only remaining logical choice was the chairman of the Presidium of the U.S.S.R. Supreme Soviet, Lukyanov. The question was: How do I get through to him?

Speaking in basic terms, there are two kinds of telephone systems in the Soviet Union. One is the regular telephone "ordinary" people use. The other is something commonly called the *vertushka,* that word coming from the verb *vertet,* to crank. It dates back to the times when one had to crank a little handle on the phone to get a connection. In the early days of Soviet government there was a special system of phone lines that only the privileged few had access to: When you "cranked" your handle, an operator would come on and you would ask her (it was always a woman) to connect you with a person or a number. As the country evolved, so did this little elitist phone system. It officially became known as the Government Communication System. At first only the very top people had it, but as the Party bureaucratic apparatus grew, the system expanded into System 1 and System 2, the former being only for the most senior officials.

Lukyanov was a System 1 person, and if I were to call him on that line (naturally, I had no such phone in my office, but I did have access to one), I would get through to him. To try to call him on his listed city number was senseless: The Government Communication System had been devised precisely to protect officials from callers, to divert ordinary callers to the ranks of secretaries whose job it was *not* to let calls through. Nevertheless, I decided to first try the regular city line.

I told the man who answered who I was and that I'd like to speak to Anatoly Ivanovich. The man asked me to call back in an hour. The old runaround, I thought to myself, but opted to wait another hour before using the "hot line." Exactly sixty minutes later I called again and—presto—I was put through. Frankly, I couldn't believe it. Lukyanov came across as very warm and wanting to be helpful. When I told him how much I wanted him on my show (I said nothing about his being a replacement for Yeltsin), he asked me to come talk to him in his office at nine in the morning. Was that okay with me? Could I make it? Did I need transportation?

This was much more than I had bargained for. Courtesy? Civility? Was I speaking to the gruff, stern, and somewhat cold Lukyanov I had seen countless times on TV chairing Supreme Soviet sessions, or was this a wrong number?

The next morning I was ushered into Lukyanov's spacious office on the fourth floor of one of the Kremlin buildings. "Anatoly Ivanovich is running a few minutes late," an aide informed me. "He asked you to forgive him." I graciously smiled and shrugged, indicating that I had indeed forgiven Anatoly Ivanovich, then sat down in one of the many armchairs at my disposal. The chairman's office was huge—one could easily ride a bike around it. But it was also cozy. There was a personal touch to it—landscapes on the walls, all depicting mountains; no official portraits, except for a large photo of Gorbachev but, again, not the official one you saw everywhere. Bookshelves lined the walls, and the books were not the usual staple of the collected works of Marx, Engels, Lenin, and Gorbachev, but included volumes of poetry and fiction.

I had about three minutes to take in these impressions. Lukyanov appeared almost out of nowhere. A part of the bookcase suddenly opened up and in he stepped. Once again I could not help but note the striking difference between the TV image and reality. On television Lukyanov came across as forceful, sly (he was nicknamed "the silver fox"), a consummate manipulator, and yet faceless, devoid of personality or presence. The Lukyanov I was now seeing was impeccably dressed in a navy blue suit that set off his silvery hair. He looked distinguished. He moved easily as he approached me, a broad smile on his tanned face. When he spoke, it was in a well modulated tone. He looked me straight in the eye. He was gracious, attentive, thanked me for having thought to invite him to do the show.

"I would love to do it, but I have a television appearance scheduled the day before your show—Mikhail Sergeyevich asked me to do it. Overexposure is not a good thing, now is it?" he asked, then continued, "But do not worry, Vladimir Vladimirovich. I will see to it that you get interesting guests. How about the speakers of both Houses? Would they suit you?" When I said they certainly would, but wondered whether they were busy, Lukyanov gave me a hint of a smile and said, "Even if they are, they will do it—if I ask them to."

And they did.

We spoke for over an hour. This man whose schedule had to be one of the busiest in the world seemed to be intent on making a good impression. He told me about what he loved most—mountain climbing (hence, the landscapes on the walls), and poetry. He was as I discovered not only an avid reader of poetry who could recite by heart from the works of Russia's greatest poets, among whom he seemed to treasure most Pasternak, he was a poet himself (a volume of his works was published shortly after that first meeting). And, as several professional poets grudgingly told me, he was in fact quite good.

He told me of his hobby—a "voice collection," several hundred tapes with recordings of readings by famous poets and writers. "I have over three hundred voices, including those of Pasternak, Mandelstam, Robert Frost, Louis Aragon," he said with obvious pride. Seeing how impressed I was (and I was indeed impressed), he told me about his "friendship" with Andrei Sakharov who, according to Lukyanov, was a moderate.

"I will always remember how Andrei Dmitriyevich sat here, in my office," reminisced Lukyanov, "and described the importance of the moderate center to which I and Gorbachev belong. He described the situation in Parliament like this: 'You,' he said, 'are like a tube of toothpaste being squeezed on either side by the Left and the Right. Slowly they are pressing out the paste that acts like a buffer and separates them. When and if they squeeze out all the paste and come together, there will be catastrophe. Your role is not to allow that.' "

I thought it was a great metaphor. But whether Lukyanov actually had a relationship with Sakharov is something I doubt. During that same conversation he referred to Stanislav Shatalin, one of the Soviet Union's most radical economists, as his friend. I was somewhat surprised because I knew Shatalin very well; his family and mine visited each other, yet I had never heard Shatalin speak of Lukyanov at all—let alone as a friend. Some time later, when I brought up that conversation, Stanislav snorted and said, "That son of a bitch! I can't stand him!"

What gradually came out was that Lukyanov was the most wonderful actor and a great psychologist. He read people like a book. He knew exactly where I came from, and he played to that. He could be everything to all people, and with me he was the intellectual liberal, the democrat, a man who could say, "Yes, we are friends with Mikhail Sergeyevich, but that does not mean I agree with everything he says or does."

A few weeks after that first meeting I interviewed Lukyanov for TV. I asked him the most difficult questions, and he fielded them skillfully. He was low-key, understanding, thoughtful, and humorous. The evening after the interview he called me at home and asked me whether I was happy with the interview, was there anything I would like to change. That was really an amazing thing to expect from a man in his position. He also asked me to call him, whenever I wanted to.

When I decided to resign from Soviet State Television—that was in April 1991—I called Lukyanov and informed him of my decision in the hope that he would ask me to explain. He did more than that—he asked me to see him first thing in the morning. When I told him about what was happening at State TV, how Gorbachev's appointee, Leonid Kravchenko, was making it impossible for anyone with integrity to work there, Lukyanov gravely shook his head, said he would talk to Gorbachev about that and begged me not to resign. Two days later Kravchenko invited me into his office and almost entreated me to take back my resignation—proof that Lukyanov had, indeed, spoken to him. I refused the offer to stay on, but that is a different story.

So that was one kind of Lukyanov. The other kind was the one who ran Politburo sessions in Gorbachev's absence and who was hard as nails and who did not have a democratic bone in his body. More will be said about that side of Lukyanov in this book, but this sketch would not be complete without two more items. One is what Russia's Prime Minister Ivan Silayev stated immediately after the coup:

"Lukyanov is the brains behind all these events."

The second pertains to a conversation between Dmitri Granin, a writer and member of Parliament, and Lukyanov. The conversation took place in September 1991, at a session of the U.S.S.R. Supreme Soviet when the delegates were castigating Lukyanov for his support of the coup. One of them called Lukyanov a modern-day Pontius Pilate. Lukyanov turned to Granin and said, "That man used to brownnose me from morning to night." Granin asked, "Anatoly Ivanovich, how can you sit here? I couldn't stand it. I would get up and leave." Lukyanov answered, "Were you present at your mother's funeral?" "Yes." "Well, this is my life's cause funeral." "What life cause?" "The Soviet Union." Lukyanov sat there in stony silence, then said: "This is the end." "The end of what?" asked Granin. "The end of the Soviet Union."

Let me repeat what I have said: None of these men were unidimensional. Most of them believed in their system of government and considered the changes engendered by *perestroika* a disaster. Yes, they acted to preserve their power, their control, their privileges. But they also acted to save their society and their country as they understood them. To deny this or not to acknowledge its importance is to misunderstand the forces that were at work over the *perestroika* years and the inevitability of what occurred between August 19 and August 21, 1991.

MONDAY, AUGUST 19, 1991

I ran, the sweet smell of late summer filling my nostrils, flooding my mouth. I ran past the rows of predominantly green-and-white little log houses of Zhukovka village, then turned left along the high iron fence of the Zhukovka-1 compound where, nearly six years of *perestroika* notwithstanding, Soviet government officials continued to live in the seclusion of their government-owned country homes, offered at ridiculously low prices. In this compound, the officials enjoyed such privileges as a private cinema theater and health club, private tennis courts, and, most desirable of all in these times of food shortages, a store that was always well stocked.

I turned right and ran on, now between two fences, the one on my left encircling another compound, Zhukovka-2, reserved for Moscow's scientific elite, the other, on my right, guarding beautiful private country homes, each one standing on about two acres of land. Another turn—right, then left—and I was passing several identical three-story pink brick mansions: Joseph Stalin's gift to the scientists who had put together the Soviet nuclear weapons project. One belonged to Andrei Sakharov. . . . A stone's throw away from it Yuri and Galina Brezhnev, son and daughter of the once all-powerful general secretary, had seen fit to build their *dachas,* while another couple of hundred yards farther down the road stood the mansion that had belonged to Mstislav Rostropovich; it was there that Alexander Solzhenitsyn had found a haven.

No matter how many times I ran past those houses (virtually every day from June to September), I could not but marvel at life's irony. An establishment scientist-turned-rebel, a dissident writer shielded by a world-class cellist who refused to back down, the children of a soon to be publicly disgraced general secretary, all living in close proximity to each other, almost certainly passing one another as they enjoyed an evening stroll. . . .

On I ran, arms swinging, legs pumping, past Sakharov, past Rostropovich, a left turn and then another and now I was heading back toward the tiny cabin that my wife and I had been renting in Zhukovka for the past four summers.

The sky was of the palest blue, meaning it could rain or shine, a most noncommittal sky, the kind mid-August brings to Moscow, a signal that autumn is coming. Now I was really flying, buoyed by the certainty that I was going to break fifteen minutes.

Now, as I think back to that Monday morning and in my mind's eye see myself running along, oblivious to the events that had begun two days earlier, I can't help but experience a sense of frustration. How could I be out there, enjoying myself, when I should have been calling out to one and all about this mortal danger? I know I was not aware of it, but that is my point: The discrepancy between those events on the one hand, and what I was doing on the other, was so great as to make me wonder whether life indeed had any meaning? That I should be running along here, enjoying myself, when not only my life, but that of a nation depended on resolute and immediate action, seemed absurd. . . .

The plotters met on Saturday, August 17, in one of the many KGB safe houses, to decide the final details, including who should fly to Foros to break the news to Gorbachev. Their choice was quite interesting.

Of the five-man delegation that arrived in Foros on Sunday, at ten minutes to five in the afternoon, only one, Oleg Baklanov, was a member of the Emergency Committee. The others represented different power structures. General Valentin Varennikov, commander of the Soviet ground forces, represented the military (Yazov would have been the better choice, but he probably refused to face Gorbachev). Lieutenant General Yuri Plekhanov, head of the KGB's Ninth Directorate, responsible for the security of all top government officials, including the president, not only spoke for the KGB but had complete access to the president's quarters. Valery Boldin, Gorbachev's chief of staff and most trusted aide, was there to convince the president to support the coup. If Boldin supported it, there was really no alternative for Gorbachev but to accept his fate—whatever it might be. Finally, the Party was represented by Central Committee Secretary Shenin. . . .

Running past the kitchen window, I waved to Katherine, who was already preparing breakfast, although it was only a quarter to seven. I jogged toward the shed where Alexei Ivanovich, the man from whom we rented our summer place, had constructed a makeshift shower. On the shed roof, filled with water, stood a large steel drum; a system of rubber hoses passed through the roof, one of them connected to a shower nozzle that hung above an old bathtub. By turning a series of handles, one could make the water flow in two directions: either to a sink or through the nozzle. There was also a wood-burning water heater, but it was never used in the summer. Depending on the weather, you took either a very cold shower or a lukewarm one.

This shower was decidedly on the cold side, so after some frenetic toweling, I dashed back to the house where I was greeted by the wonderful smell of frying tomatoes, eggs, and steaming espresso. I switched on the television set to catch the morning news. The screen lit up and I saw Soviet television's star announcer, Yuri Petrov, sitting at a desk and reading something official. Without even realizing it, I was immediately struck by two things: Yuri's color and the tone of his voice. Perhaps the best way to describe it is to say there was none. He had no color, he was white, and he had no voice; instead of his resonant baritone, I was hearing something flat, something that sounded dead. Then the words began to register:

". . . Having taken advantage of the freedom they have been given, trampling the first shoots of democracy, extremist forces have adopted a course aimed at liquidating the Soviet Union, destroying the State and taking over power at any cost. They have disregarded the results of the national referendum on our homeland's unity. Their cynical speculations as they play on national feelings are nothing but a screen set up to satisfy their ambitions.

"Neither the present hardships of their people, nor their tomorrow, concern these political adventurists. Having created an atmosphere of moral and political terror and attempting to hide behind a shield of popular trust, they forget that the ties they condemn and try to break are the result of a far greater popular support which, what's more, has been tested by many centuries of history. Today those who in essence work to overthrow the constitutional government must answer to mothers and fathers for the death of many hundreds of victims of intranational strife. The wrecked lives of over half a million refugees are on their heads. It is because of them that tens of millions of Soviet people who only yesterday lived as one family have now lost both peace and happiness, for they find themselves unwanted in their own home.

"Only the people can decide the social system, yet that right is being taken away from them."

Petrov read on in that flat unemotional tone, the words, like unintelligible pieces of a jigsaw puzzle, falling into place and bringing back a different time, a time I thought was gone forever, a time that stifled your breath and froze your soul:

"The deepening destabilization of the political and economic situation in the Soviet Union is undermining our international standing. Here and there we begin to hear calls for revenge, for reviewing our borders. Some even call for dismantling of the Soviet Union and for instituting some form of international trusteeship over parts and regions of the country. Such is the bitter reality. Only yesterday a Soviet citizen, when abroad, felt himself to be a worthy representative of an influential and respected country. Nowadays he is often no more than a second-

class foreigner with whom one deals with condescension
or sympathy.''

I found that I was cold, so cold that I was shaking.
Katherine stood beside me repeating just two words: ''My
God, My God, My God . . .''

Neither of us had the slightest doubt about what had
happened. We had spoken about the danger of a coup
many times, I, as usual, not denying it could happen, but
arguing how remote the possibility seemed to me. Katherine told me to wake up to reality, always expecting the
worst, sometimes telling me she did this just to hear me
respond and that way bolster her hopes.

Our first real argument about the possibility of a right-
wing coup dated back four years and had been touched
off by what probably still stands as the single most debated publication of the entire *perestroika* period. Written
in the form of an open letter and signed by one Nina
Andreyeva, it took up one full newspaper page. It had
been the first real signal of a hard-line move to stop *perestroika*.

Flashback: The Principles of Nina Andreyeva

By the fall of 1991, if anything had changed over the five-
plus years of Gorbachev's *perestroika,* it was the media. Soviet journalists had always been considered part of the vast
army referred to as "fighting men of the ideological front."
As one might paraphrase Tennyson, theirs was not to question why, theirs was but to write or die.

There is some exaggeration to that phrase, for it suggests
that journalists in the Soviet Union were forced to write—
which is not the case. The majority of them, just like the
majority of the people, believed in their system—yes, with

certain qualifications; yes, some believed it more, some less; yes, at times looking the other way. But, nevertheless, they were true believers. In most cases when they criticized (and they did, provided the criticism was not a generalization and did not concern people of a certain standing), their aim was to *improve* their society, to *do away* with its shortcomings, to *help attain* the cherished goals of a socialist society.

Today that support of the system may be denied by many, but even up to 1985 and the advent of Gorbachev, even after the corruption of nearly nineteen years of Brezhnev, even after cynicism might have seemed the only lifesaver by which to stay afloat, idealism remained very much part of the journalistic outlook. And so, when Gorbachev announced the birth of *glasnost,* he found a far more eager and responsive audience in the journalistic profession than, say, in the political or economic areas, when he called for *perestroika,* that is, "restructuring."

But that is not all. For those who were part of the political-economic structure, *perestroika* was a devastating threat. Restructuring meant they would no longer be able to control the country through the complex system of levers of what later came to be called the Command-Administrative System. Not so the journalists. *Glasnost* meant freedom, it meant being able, at long last, to write without any internal censor grabbing your most sensitive parts and giving them a sharp tug that set off every alarm bell in your system. It meant not having to submit your text to a real censor. And it meant, most importantly, regaining your feeling of self-respect and being able to write or say everything, or just about everything you wanted to say about *any*thing, or almost anything.

Overnight, journalists became heroes. Newspapers, magazines, certain TV shows took center stage. Radical, extremist, centrist—all of it was there. Sometimes probing and intelligent, sometimes outrageous and irresponsible, almost always irreverent and outspoken, the media was like a blast of fresh air in a stifling room.

Magazines and dailies that had hardly enjoyed popularity in the past, such as the weekly *Ogonyok* and *Moskovskiye Novosty,* suddenly became the hottest articles in the country, their circulation increasing at times by a factor of ten and more. Others began to sink, among them such publications as the seemingly sacrosanct *Pravda.*

Gradually, as the divisions in Soviet society deepened, different publications began to represent the views and desires of certain groups. Where they had once been banners, they now became standard bearers. The political polarization of the media was a gradual process that began slowly, then gathered strength, and finally exploded onto everyone's consciousness with the publication of what came to be called the Anti-*perestroika* Manifesto, a major fullpage article which appeared in the March 19, 1987, issue of *Sovetskaya Rossiya,* a national daily published by the Central Committee. The article, signed by Nina Andreyeva, an obscure chemistry teacher from Leningrad, bore the title "I Cannot Abandon My Principles."

I remember first seeing that article on a plane as I was flying home to Moscow from New York. Two things struck me then. One was the tone and content. They whisked me back three years, they erased everything that had happened since April 1985, they appealed to and played on every thought and sentiment that had been ingrained in every one of us who had lived under Brezhnev, under Khrushchev, under Stalin. The other was the sudden realization on my part that Nina Andreyeva's rallying cry had appeared when Gorbachev was away, in Yugoslavia. Later, that pattern would be repeated time and again, up to and including the coup itself, but back then there was still no pattern. I also remember asking myself who was this Andreyeva woman, this chemistry teacher who seemed intimately familiar with not only the writings of Marx, but with those of many other philosophers as well?

Interestingly enough, *not one major newspaper, not a single magazine,* had the courage to respond. The past still hung heavy over all of us. No editor was yet prepared to take on the establishment—and no one doubted Nina Andreyeva's Stalinist sermon had the establishment's blessing. That this was indeed the case was made clear when Yegor Ligachev, then the number-two man in the Party hierarchy, convened a special meeting. In no uncertain terms, he informed the editors of all major publications, along with the chairmen of Soviet State TV and radio and Tass, the official Soviet wire service, that Nina Andreyeva's letter (the article had been written in that form) was a model to be emulated by the media.

It was not only a model, it was also a signal to all the anti-*perestroika* forces. A few days after that publication, I spoke at the House of Actors, a club frequented mainly by people from the world of theater. After the speech, during the Q & A, I began to receive written questions signed "A Russian worker," "an ordinary proletarian," and the like. The questions were ferociously anti-Semitic, Stalinist, and hate mongering. I challenged their author—clearly, they came from one source—to get up and be recognized, but got no response.

But the author did make himself known later—in a very ironic way. After the Q & A, I went to have a cup of tea with some of the people who had organized the evening. My wife had said she would join us in a few minutes. The minutes soon became more like half an hour, and by the time she finally appeared I was getting somewhat impatient, a fact I did not hesitate to make known. But when she explained the reasons for her delay, my impatience turned into amazement.

"As I was standing there smoking," she said, "this small, balding man came up to me and asked, 'What is a Russian blond beauty like you doing in this "synagogue"?' When I told him I enjoyed listening to your speeches, he became very agitated. He told me you were part of a Zionist plot to destroy Russia. Naturally, I did not tell him you were my husband. I feigned total surprise at what he said and asked him to tell me more. And he did. Much more.

"He told me he was part of a nationwide organization called Pamyat, an organization of Russian patriots. He told me they were exceptionally well organized. That they were structured in groups of tens, hundreds, thousands, and something he called 'blacknesses'—units that are ten thousand strong. Each of these groups has a commander who reports to one and only one superior. Ten commanders of a Ten Group report to one commander of a Hundred Group. Ten Hundred-Group commanders report to one commander of a Thousand Group. I asked him if there was a supreme commander. He gave me a very sly look and said, 'We are not just well organized, we have very strong support in very high places.' And when I asked him what kind of support, he said, 'Ligachev.' He then told me how they would give Russia back to the Russians, get rid of all the Marxist kikes who had betrayed Russia and were betraying it today. When I told him he did not look very Russian to me, he got angry and said he was half Georgian and half Russian by birth, but that in his heart he was all Russian."

As we later discovered, this man was none other than Smirnov-Ostashvili, one of Pamyat's most vitriolic anti-Semites, in a certain sense an historical figure: In 1990 he led a group that disrupted a meeting of writers, most of whom were Jewish. Thanks to someone's having had a camcorder, his anti-Semitic insults were recorded on tape. That led to his being taken to court for overt anti-Semitism and sentenced to two years in prison. This was the first time ever (and still stands as the only time) that anyone in the Soviet Union was punished for statements and activities aimed against an ethnic or religious minority, in this case,

Jews. (I might also say, in passing, that I know of no other *country* where anyone has been incarcerated for that crime.) Smirnov-Ostashvili later hanged himself in prison. I believe he was mentally unstable and actually believed the things he said. He must have thought the anti-Russian plot he so feared had triumphed, so he had no more reason to live. A pathetic case, except for that one revelation: "Ligachev supports us."

In the battle against change, against *perestroika*, Ligachev (and others, as we shall see) were ready to do just about anything and support just about anybody—be it a crazed anti-Semite like Smirnov-Ostashvili, or a fanatical Stalinist like Nina Andreyeva. After the failure of the coup, Alexander N. Yakovlev, initially Gorbachev's mentor (something that did not stop Gorbachev from dropping him when he considered it to be politically expedient), made the following statement during a television interview:

"Gorbachev was in Yugoslavia, I was in Mongolia. As soon as I read that 'letter,' I immediately understood everything. After all, I know how the apparatus functions; it was clear to me that such a publication had to be cleared at the very highest level (in Gorbachev's absence only Ligachev could grant such sanctions). What that letter represented was a harsh command: 'Stop!'

"Mikhail Sergeyevich returned three days later. Immediately he started getting phone calls from editors asking him what to do. . . . I began to look into what this was all about and discovered that some people had been dispatched to Leningrad to work with Andreyeva on her letter —one was the head of the science department of *Sovetskaya Rossiya,* a man conversant in philosophy. I also learned that the Secretariat of the Central Committee had been convened by Ligachev specifically to support that project. Gorbachev called a Politburo meeting and, thank God, let them have it right between the eyes.

"After that, things went the way they always have: The

Politburo took a vote and everyone voted to publish a reply to the Andreyeva piece. Soon after that [on April 5, 1987] we published an article in *Pravda* where we called the *Sovetskaya Rossiya* article an anti-*perestroika* manifesto.

"The next thing we knew, letters began to appear in local newspapers around the country attacking me for being too liberal with the media. A whole wave of letters came to the Central Committee denouncing the *Pravda* piece, followed by resolutions sent in by Party committees endorsing *Sovetskaya Rossiya*. What we did not know then was that all of those letters carried by the local press, all of those protests sent to the Central Committee, all of those Party meetings were the result of a series of phone calls from the pro-Ligachev faction of the Central Committee who demanded that all local Party organizations support the Andreyeva article. Finally, because of the heat this issue generated, Gorbachev decided to relieve both Ligachev and myself from the ideological duties we had been given as Central Committee secretaries."

I remember how happy I was when Yakovlev became the Party's man for foreign relations, whereas Ligachev was moved to one of the most impossibly difficult areas—agriculture. I remember gloating at the prospects of Ligachev's breaking his neck trying to solve what no one before him had been able to improve. I chuckled at what seemed to me to be a master stroke on Gorbachev's part. Little did I know . . .

By the spring of 1987 people were actively beginning to take sides. Prior to that, Gorbachev's policies had not really been clear. Most people saw him much more as a fixer than as a reformer, meaning he was someone who was trying to improve the system rather than change it. As long as that was the case, Soviet society and especially its top echelons remained monolithic. But when Gorbachev first showed his hand, shortly after the Twenty-seventh Congress of the Communist Party of the Soviet Union in the late winter of

1986, when the country's power structure began to comprehend that *perestroika* meant much more than "rebuilding," and that Gorbachev was proposing radical change though he was calling it something much less disconcerting, there began a process of polarization that was to continue up until the coup itself.

At the initial stages of this schism, both sides had their leaders. Later, as Soviet society raced helter-skelter toward its destiny, the original two groups would splinter into scores of parties, societies, and associations, each with its own "top gun." At times the differences between them would blur—what with old hard-line Communist Party conservatives, neo-Marxist conservatives, Democratic Communist Party conservatives, monarchists, and scores of others vying for leadership in the anti-Gorbachev movement. The same applies to the liberals. But, as I noted, at the beginning the lines were sharper and the distinctions were clear. This was not only because the process was in its formative period, but was also due, to no less a degree, to two men who embodied the different sides so perfectly: Yegor Ligachev and Alexander Yakovlev.

I have been fortunate enough to have known both of them, seen them in action, and experienced their personalities.

If the Party had been able to create in laboratory conditions its model human being, Yegor Ligachev would have been that person. He was the prototype of the Party worker par excellence, the quintessential Communist as described in high school textbooks. To begin with, he was physically perfect: Neither too big nor too small, too fat nor too thin, he had an attractive yet not overly handsome face, piercing blue eyes, and white hair rising in a crest above a high forehead. Ligachev was the perfect fit for what might be called "a man of the people," or what in Soviet Party speech was referred to as "a simple person." (In this case the word "simple" meant "ordinary," that is, "one of us," one of the

"real people," not an effete intellectual.) But it was not just
a matter of the man's physique. It was a matter of
Ligachev's presence, of his bearing—the squared shoulders,
the ramrod-straight back, the firm handshake, the determined stride—and, most of all, his speech. It was always
clear, the voice of everyman, but a passionate voice, a voice
full of fire, the voice of a cheerleader. This man who had
come to Moscow by the way of the Siberian city of Tomsk,
where he had made a reputation for himself as a "just tsar,"
was the walking, talking, exact image of the model that Stalin's society had been able to create. Some of the models
had been botched, others lacked this or that ingredient, but
Yegor Ligachev had it all.

Was he a true believer or did he just mouth the words?
Was he honest or was he a hypocrite? Did he care about the
people or was his only interest personal? As paradoxical as
it may seem, the answer to all these questions is yes.

It is tempting and oh-so-easy to treat Ligachev like some
kind of arch-villain, the sterotypical hard-line Communist
boss whose boorish persona has figured for so many years in
the United States media. My readers would swallow yet another description of that sort without even noticing it, let
alone needing a glass of water (or something stronger) with
which to get it down. If all the Central Committee's members had simply been dark knights of an evil empire, *perestroika* would have been infinitely easier to accomplish, for
these men would have had no support from the people.

Yes, Ligachev was a consummate hypocrite, a man who,
like few others, was skilled in behind-the-scenes deals and
intrigue. Yes, he was power-hungry, more than ready to say
whatever he thought would serve his political interests. Yes,
he was cunning and dangerous, one of Gorbachev's most
dangerous opponents in those early days. But he was also
fighting for a system he truly supported. If the system had
not worked elsewhere, said Ligachev, that was not because
of some innate deficiency, it was because of people—some

inept, others dishonest. But that was not socialism's fault. Ligachev could—and did—point to Tomsk and to the Tomsk region and say with pride: "Look what I achieved." While this gave rise to many jokes about building socialism in one separate city (a takeoff on Lenin's proposal to build socialism in one separate country, something Marx had called unrealistic), it is nonetheless true that Ligachev's tenure as first secretary of the Tomsk Regional Party Committee was marked with successes in such varied areas as the improvement of housing, distribution, crime fighting, agriculture, and cultural development.

Ligachev certainly wanted change for Soviet society, but he wanted the kind of change that would preserve the Party's power and preeminence, preserve the Union, and preserve socialism as he understood that idea. Ligachev wanted to do away with the conditions that spawned apathy, corruption, and crime. He was a Stalinist—not in his desire to restore the gulag, but in his firm belief in centralized power, public ownership, collective farming, and a one-party system. And it was this belief, these principles, that made Ligachev the true leader of the Soviet conservative movement.

The contrast between Ligachev and Alexander Yakovlev was almost anecdotal in its completeness. Where one sported a wave of white hair, the other had a monklike tonsure; where one had bright blue eyes, the other had dark brown ones; where Ligachev's delivery was fiery and his posture akin to that of a Prussian officer, Yakovlev spoke in subdued tones, walked with the hint of a limp, and had a tendency to slouch. Contrasting as those features were, they really only accentuated the profound ideological differences between these two men.

Yakovlev was indeed "a simple person"; born into a peasant family in a small Russian village in the mid 1920s, he took advantage of what the Bolshevik Revolution gave to so many people like him: He got himself a high school educa-

tion and then, after World War II (during which he fought
and was seriously wounded), acquired a university education. He was included in the first-ever group of Soviet graduate students to be sent to the United States—that was in
1959—where he studied for one year at Columbia University. While the time spent in New York must certainly have
been an eye-opener, Alexander Yakovlev returned to the
Soviet Union as convinced of the superiority of the Soviet
socialist system as when he had arrived in America a year
earlier. Offered a Party job, he moved up through the ranks
and soon achieved senior status. But Yakovlev was far too
independent a thinker to last long in an environment that
demanded conformity.

In 1972 he published a major article in a national weekly
(the *Literaturnaya Gazeta*), in which he not only took anti-
Semites to task, but decried anti-Semitism, particularly in
Russia. To my knowledge, this was the first time anyone in
the Soviet Union, especially a ranking Party official, had
ever acknowledged the existence of that shameful prejudice
in the country. But Yakovlev did much more than acknowledge it. He described the consequences of anti-Semitism for
Russia, such as the emigration of Jews, the loss of some of
the country's best and brightest. He also wrote eloquently
about the Jewish contribution to Russian culture and the
special role played by the intelligentsia.

Yakovlev had done the impermissible. Instead of singing
the praises of the proletariat, instead of celebrating the
friendship of the peoples of the Soviet Union, he had per-
mitted himself to be critical of these two cornerstones of the
Soviet edifice. Retribution was unavoidable. It came to him
in the shape of banishment to the largely ceremonial post of
Soviet ambassador to Canada. It was there, in Ottawa, that
I first met Yakovlev in 1979, when he summoned me from
Toronto, where I had appeared in a series of television debates. I will never forget how impressed I was by this man. It
was not that he had charisma; rather, it was a spell cast by

his intelligence, by the keen wit you saw in his eyes, by the subdued thoughtfulness of everything he said. There was something homey about him—you had the feeling of being in the presence of a terribly wise man who was sitting there in his slippers and in an old woolen vest sharing his thoughts with you. And the wonderful thing about his intelligence was that, far from intimidating you, it made you feel more intelligent.

A few years later—I believe it was in 1983—Mikhail Gorbachev, then secretary of the Party for agriculture—came to Canada on an official visit. Naturally, he was greeted by Ambassador Yakovlev to whom, the story goes, he showed a copy of the speech he was going to deliver the next day. Yakovlev took the speech and did something both unusual and unthinkable as far as the Soviet diplomatic establishment was concerned: He read the speech and told Gorbachev it was terrible and had to be rewritten.

One must understand the almost unlimited power of a Politburo member to realize what kind of danger Yakovlev was exposing himself to. Already a man out of favor with the establishment, he was playing a game of political double or nothing by telling Gorbachev he had written a weak speech. Better said, he was not playing any games at all—he was doing what he had always done, he was being honest. And highly conscientious, for he then presented Gorbachev with the revised copy of the speech that he had written. To Gorbachev's credit, he accepted Yakovlev's version. The speech was a major success. From that day on, Yakovlev came to occupy a very special place in Gorbachev's heart and mind. When Gorbachev became general secretary two years later, he brought Yakovlev back to Moscow as both confidant and closest adviser.

There is no doubt that Yakovlev was *perestroika*'s principle architect, a man who had the courage to question his deepest convictions and unflinchingly admit his mistakes.

Of all the men who surrounded Gorbachev, he was—and remains—the most honest and the least self-centered.

If the article in *Sovetskaya Rossiya* was the first shot, or rather blast, in the media battle against Gorbachev and *perestroika,* it was far from the last. Such periodicals as the monthly *Molodaya Gvardia* and *Nash Sovremennik,* such weeklies and dailies as *Literaturnaya Rossiya, Glasnost,* and *Den* did not hesitate to carry everything from the most obnoxious attacks on known *perestroika* leaders to blatant calls for vigilance in the struggle against the "Zionist-Masonic plot." As a matter of fact, a few days after the coup had failed, I received reports from certain sources informing me that some staff people in the Central Committee had actually seen mock-ups of front-page articles slated for publication in *Sovetskaya Rossiya* and other "loyal" papers, announcing that a Zionist-Masonic group had been apprehended just hours before an attempt to overthrow the legal government. Needless to say, all of these plotters were people close to Gorbachev. . . .

But perhaps Ligachev's sinister role was best demonstrated by yet another post-coup revelation, namely, that his closest aide, one Valery Legostayev, had been the principal author of Nina Andreyeva's "letter." Many Central Committee staff members had been aware of his work on this "manifesto" which, when approved by his boss, Ligachev, was taken to Leningrad by a courier (the head of the newspaper's science department), signed by Ms. Andreyeva, and then published.

Why, when Gorbachev was informed of these matters, as he surely must have been almost immediately, did he not get rid of Ligachev, force him into retirement, as had become the traditional way of dealing with political opponents? Probably because in March–April of 1987 Gorbachev did not believe he had sufficient power to do so. The old structures were still intact. There had, as yet, been no general elections to the Supreme Soviet, and no local elections. There was still only one political party and it controlled every facet of life, as it had for over seventy years. Gorbachev was probably right in that assessment. He may also have been right in taking ideology—that is, the entire media—out of the hands of both Ligachev *and* Yakovlev. By doing that he was defusing whatever ammunition the far Right could have used to accuse him of playing the game of favoritism.

But he was definitely wrong when he gradually began to side with the right wing against the liberal media. For journalists it was a frustrating and, at the same time, fascinating experience.

It was, after all, Gorbachev who had liberated the media. He expected it to be "truthful" and "objective," which, of course, implied the duty of journalists to investigate and criticize. What he did not expect was that he could become a target for critical fire. It would not be inconceivable for Gorbachev the theoretician of *glasnost* to clash with Gorbachev the practical politician: No general secretary of the Communist Party had ever been criticized by the press with impunity, and though he might have accepted the notion that it could happen in principle, he could not deal with it when it actually occurred. And then there was also the issue of hurt feelings: How dare you bite the very hand that liberated you!

In the fall of 1989, Vladislav Starkov, the editor of *Argumenty y Fakty,* one of the most pro-*perestroika* and outspoken weeklies, published the results of a public opinion poll showing that Gorbachev's popularity had dropped dramatically and was far lower than that of Andrei Sakharov and of Gorbachev's arch rival Boris Yeltsin. Retaliation was swift and, in some ways, a reminder of days past. Gorbachev publicly gave Starkov a dressing down and said, "If I were you, I would resign."

A day or so later Starkov was summoned by Gorbachev's new ideological appointee, Vadim Medvedev, who advised him to give up his editorship. As Starkov related the story to me, Medvedev was almost apologetic, promising him a very nice job in some other nonjournalistic capacity. But Starkov point blank refused to play by the old rules and promised to raise a holy stink if any more pressure was put on him.

It was then that I decided to invite Starkov to be a guest on my show *An Evening with Vladimir Pozner.* The subject of discussion would be freedom of the press. However, before inviting Starkov I decided to inform the editor of the Moscow TV department, which produced my show, about my intention. The editor's reaction was typical: "I cannot give you permission to do that. If any of the vice chairmen give you the green light, you have my full support. But if not, and if you go ahead and put him on, they will hold me responsible."

The vice chairman for television was one Piotr Reshetov, a man who had been brought into that position for just one purpose: to cut off heads. The chairman, Mikhail Nenashev, formerly head of the State Publishing Committee, relied on Reshetov to do his dirty work for him—and he did it. Our conversation was brief and to the point: I would not be allowed to put Starkov on because that would be seen as a public affront to Gorbachev on the part of Gosteleradio— as the State Committee for Television and Radio was usually referred to. The best I could do was send Starkov a telegram informing him I would join his staff to go on strike if he was removed from office.

Starkov survived and his paper has flourished—a very basic departure from times when even a scowl on the part of the general secretary would have led to his dismissal and could have led to something far worse. Gorbachev clearly lost face as a result of that confrontation, but he refused to learn that lesson. He continued to criticize the press, especially the progressive, democratic press, thereby echoing the views of the most reactionary members of the Central Committee and the Supreme Soviet. He even went so far as to call for temporarily repealing the Press Law—that occurred in November of 1990, when the president seemed to have decided to throw in his lot with the hard-liners.

It was also at that time that Gorbachev very effectively took over personal control of Gosteleradio. He had been particularly unhappy with television—not because it was outspokenly critical of his policies (it was certainly not), but because it was not, in his view, sufficiently supportive of him. Broadcasting over eleven time zones and addressing a potential audience of over two hundred million people, Soviet television was by far the most influential force of the media. Prior to *perestroika,* heads of television were formally appointed by the prime minister but in fact were chosen by the Politburo. That had been the case with the first three chairmen under whom I had worked—Mesiatsev, Lapin, and Aksionov. Once democratic general elections to the Soviet Parliament were held, a new system was adopted: The chairman of the Supreme Soviet (later, the president of the U.S.S.R.) nominated all Cabinet members, the chairman of TV included, and the Supreme Soviet either endorsed that person or not. Thus, Mikhail Nenashev became the first chairman of Soviet TV whose candidacy was actually debated in a public forum.

Still, Gorbachev was not satisfied. In the late fall of 1990 he came up with a very crafty plan: transform the Soviet TV and Radio Committee into a State *company,* thereby excluding its chairman from the Cabinet. Once that happened, there would no longer be any need to seek the Supreme Soviet's consent. Thus, "presidential" television was born with the appointment of Leonid Kravchenko.

Gorbachev's choice was, to say the least, interesting. In fact, it represented a major policy outlook change.

By the time of his appointment to this key post, Kravchenko was still a relatively young man (he was in his early fifties) who had covered a lot of ground. A graduate of Moscow University's prestigious Department of Journalism, he had moved steadily up through the ranks, combining Young Communist League and Party activities with journalism. A bright and charming man, whose boyish face belied his cunning mind, Kravchenko was spectacularly successful wherever he went. As editor, he turned the official trade union daily *Trud,* which virtually no one looked at, into the most widely read newspaper in the Soviet Union, surpassing both *Pravda* and *Izvestia* in circulation. I first met him in 1986, when he was appointed to serve as deputy to the new chairman, Alexander Aksionov. I remember how charmed I was during that first encounter, how high were my hopes. Kravchenko said all the right things. He seemed to read my mind and said exactly what I wanted to hear—that was, as many of us were soon to learn, one of his greatest assets.

Soon, however, the charm began to wear off. And then finally came the day when we all understood where Kravchenko really stood. This occurred just shortly before the Andreyeva affair, when Ligachev was still head of ideology. One day, he came to visit Gosteleradio—a visit that would take him to the news department, the public affairs department, the youth department and, finally, a meeting with the committee's management and leading journalists. At that meeting I saw how Kravchenko literally hung on Ligachev's every word—he was, beyond a doubt, pro-Ligachev. Automatically, that made him anti-Gorbachev. When Kravchenko was relieved of his duties in 1988 and appointed to head Tass, most of us at television heaved a sigh of relief. But when he was personally appointed to head television in the fall of 1990, we perceived it as a catastrophe. His initial statement was, to say the least, straightforward: "I am the president's man and I have come to carry out the president's will. I do not care what your politics are. I care only about how good you are at your job and about your integrity. I have no other concerns." In fact, only the first sentence had any truth to it.

Between his appointment in November 1990, and the

coup of August 1991, Kravchenko fired scores of people, forced others to leave, and took several of the most popular shows off the air—all of this on purely *political grounds.* He got rid of the most highly regarded journalists, the most professional, those with the most integrity.

In March of 1991, after returning from a trip to the United States, I was informed by one of Kravchenko's deputies that I was in trouble. According to a report that he had been handed, I had stated certain "unacceptable" things when I was a guest on *The Joan Rivers Show.* According to the report (which was quite truthful), I had said, among many other things, that President Gorbachev enjoyed very little popularity in his own country, that Americans had misread him and continued to do so, that, finally, the most respected political figure in the Soviet Union today was Boris Yeltsin—and I would vote for him, not for Gorbachev. According to what I was told, Kravchenko's reaction to what I had said was to ask, "I wonder whether there is any room for Pozner in our organization?" By that time I had already decided there was not, and so I tendered my resignation, which was formally accepted on April 15.

Kravchenko's appointment was a disaster. It lead to the virtual breakdown of television, it forced the best people to leave—and this was supposedly because Kravchenko wanted to see to it that the president's will was respected. Gorbachev has never explained why he made that choice, why he continued to stand behind Kravchenko up until the coup itself. During those three days Kravchenko fully supported the new leadership. Not that he could have put on different programming: The TV Center was occupied, there were armed soldiers on every floor and in front of every studio. But he could have walked away from his job, could have gone over to Yeltsin. . . . Then again, he probably couldn't because by August he was one of the most hated men in the entire country; for him there was really no going back. He was, in reality, a Ligachev man, a man who, I am sure, secretly applauded Nina Andreyeva's notorious letter and who shared the same principles as those who orchestrated that first blow against *perestroika:* to stay in power, to preserve the system—no matter what lies, deception, and even bloodshed it might take to do it.

Yuri Petrov finished reading. He looked up from his text (most Soviet announcers do not use a TelePrompTer) and intoned, ". . . signed by the State Committee for the State of Emergency in the U.S.S.R." The screen went blank for a few seconds and then came to life with scenes of the Bolshoi Ballet doing *Swan Lake.* There was something surrealistic in juxtaposing Tchaikovsky's music and the dancing figures of the lady swans gracefully moving hither and yon with the toneless voice and vacant eyes of Yuri Petrov reading "The Appeal to the Soviet People."

I rapidly threw on my clothes and we sat down for a quick breakfast. I don't think either of us noticed the taste of what we ate or drank. Nor did we speak. There was really nothing to say. I recall hoping Katherine would just keep quiet, not ask me what to do —the idea of trying to come up with any kind of answer was unbearable. I had no answer. Just one thought pulsated through my head: "This is the end. It's all over. We are all dead."

The screen went blank again, then Yuri Petrov reappeared, looked at us hopelessly and read:

"Statement of the Chairman of the U.S.S.R. Supreme Soviet:

"Due to the multitude of requests I have been receiving from working people asking that I state my views concerning the published draft of the Union treaty, I feel it necessary to emphasize . . ." And on and on, about how poorly the draft treaty had been prepared by Gorbachev, Yeltsin, and the other presidents of the republics; how they had ignored the will of the Soviet people, expressed in a referendum that the Union of Soviet Socialist Republics be preserved; how they had ignored the Supreme Soviet's recommendations on many economic and legal issues. The statement was signed August 16, 1991, by Anatoly Lukyanov.

Lukyanov? Gorbachev's friend of thirty-five years? The man who had stood at his side from day one of *perestroika,* steadfastly supporting him? Unbelievable. And, if that statement was signed August 16, why was it being read only now, on August 19?

Three days later I discovered the answer to that question. Lukyanov's statement first appeared in print in *Izvestia*—the newspaper published by the very same Supreme Soviet of which Lukyanov was the chairman. For well over a year the *Izvestia* staff had been demanding a change in editorship. The paper unanimously supported Igor Golembiovsky, one of the deputy editors and a radical reformist, while Lukyanov supported his appointee Nikolai Yefimov, a hard-line communist. Yefimov owed Lukyanov—and he did what he could to repay that debt. The original of Lukyanov's handwritten statement differed from the one published in *Izvestia* and read on television in only one detail: Whereas the latter speaks about "the published draft of the Union treaty," the original refers to "the draft of the Union treaty, published three days ago." Insignificant? On the contrary, extremely important.

The draft of the Union treaty was published in all Soviet national dailies *on August 15.* "Three days ago" meant that Lukyanov had written his statement *on August 18, not on August 16.* It meant that he had written it not *before,* and therefore independently of, the coup, but *after* Mikhail Gorbachev had been forced to receive a delegation from Moscow on the afternoon of August 18, had refused to sign a document approving the intention to announce a state of emergency in the country, and had been put under house arrest. By omitting the words "three days ago," Yefimov made it seem as if Lukyanov's statement had nothing to do with the coup; had the original not been found, Lukyanov would have had an ironclad alibi. . . .

Yuri Petrov was reading again. *Swan Lake* had flickered back onto the screen, then melted away. Now Petrov was reading "The Statement of the Soviet Leadership." It announced that "because of health problems" incapacitating Mikhail Sergeyevich Gorbachev, U.S.S.R. vice president Gennadi Yanayev would be taking over his responsibilities.

My wife and I looked at each other. "The bastards have killed Gorbachev," I said, and I felt rage boiling up in me, rage at and pity for this man who had started it all, who had broken with the past, who had given us all so much hope, changed our lives, but had yet somehow not had the courage, or the foresight, or the determination to go all the way and had backed off and cast his lot with the unspeakable swine who had now killed him and taken over. I could almost see his face, the eyes closed, the bullet hole in his forehead right next to the famous birthmark, the blood trickling over his face, and I wanted to scream at that dead face "Idiot! Idiot! Idiot! We told you so! We warned you, you sorrowful son of a bitch! Now look what you've done!" And I wanted to cry tears of complete frustration.

". . . Third. To govern the country and make the state of emergency measures effective, a State Committee for the State of Emergency in the U.S.S.R. (SCSE U.S.S.R.) shall be formed . . ." We listened to the names as one would listen to a prison sentence: Baklanov, deputy chairman of the U.S.S.R. Defense Council; Kryuchkov, chairman of the KGB; Prime Minister Pavlov; chief of police Pugo; Starodubtsev, head of the so-called Peasants' Union; Tizyakov, president of an industrial association

representing the defense industries; Vice President Yanayev; Defense Minister Yazov. Not one even remotely liberal face. Not one.

Tchaikovsky was back again with *Swan Lake.* And that
would go on all day. News bulletins, announcers reading
the Emergency Committee's "statements" and "direc-
tives," and then *Swan Lake.* I didn't realize it then, but for
many people Tchaikovsky's masterpiece will never spark
any emotion except the sickening feeling of despair we
felt that Monday morning.

Katherine and I got into the car and drove back to Moscow. It was about a quarter to eight. The winding Uspen-
sky Road was its usual self, the traffic was still light, the
woods and fields spreading left and right were still lush.
We drove silently, both steeped in our own thoughts, yet
both communicating. We reached the Mozhaisk Highway
in about fifteen minutes.

"Look," I said, "tanks."

"Where? Where?" asked Katherine, and I could hear
the notes of fear in her voice. I tilted my jaw in the general
direction of the huge, somewhat obscene machines.
Cannon snouts pointing forward and up, they rolled along
on the edge of the highway, indifferent and yet terribly
threatening.

What we were seeing was the result of what had happened after the five-man delegation had returned from
the Crimea and reported to Yanayev and company about
Gorbachev's refusal to go along with the coup. After a
short meeting on Sunday night, the plotters began operations.

At 4 A.M. on Monday morning Vice President Gennadi
Yanayev officially declared a state of emergency in some
parts of the country and assumed the presidency. Half an
hour later, Defense Minister Yazov dispatched Coded Telegram 8825 ordering the armed forces all over the country to alert status. Simultaneously the Taman Guards, the

Kantemirovsky Mechanized and the Ryazan Airborne—three crack divisions—were sent into Moscow to occupy strategic points.

At 6 A.M. Yazov convened a meeting of his top military commanders in the Defense Ministry building. None of them—this was confirmed later—had any information about the coup. Nor did they get any now. Yazov told them he wanted "no stupid actions, no bloodshed." Just order.

"What will happen to Peter?" asked Katherine.

Our son had just spent ten weeks in Atlanta as part of an exchange between Soviet TV, where he worked as a commentator, and CNN. Today he was in New York, scheduled to board a plane for Moscow in the late afternoon.

"You want him to stay over there?" I asked.

"Yes. I would like that."

"I'm not sure that's possible. I mean, his visa is probably not valid after the nineteenth."

"You have friends in Washington. Call them. At least if Peter stays put, there is some hope."

We drove down Kutuzovsky Prospect, then over the bridge, leaving the Russian Federation government building on our right, up to the Garden Ring road. Everything seemed to be as usual. We made a right, passed the wedding-cake building of the Ministry of Foreign Affairs, made a U-turn and a right into Shchukin Street. In less than a minute we would arrive at the large and somewhat ornate archway to our apartment building. I would drive through it and then park in the yard directly under one of the five windows of our apartment. As we approached, I found myself thinking: "Will they be there waiting for me? Will I spot them before I drive into the yard? What do I do if I see a suspicious black Volga parked in front of the Patriarch's residence? What then? What do I do, if they are there? Do I try to get away?"

The main office and the residence of the Patriarch of the Russian Orthodox Church are situated exactly opposite my house. They are guarded round the clock by the police, much like any of the foreign embassies in Moscow, but also differing from embassies by having their own private security. Over the years—Katherine and I had been living here since 1975—I had gotten to know the Patriarch's people. Whenever they had the chance, they would question me about politics, about what the Soviet government was doing, about the United States—in short, I was their "expert" on political affairs. As I became more and more outspokenly critical of the government, especially in Brezhnev's later years, followed by Andropov and Chernenko, some of these young men had jokingly told me that if things got bad for me, I could always count on them for sanctuary.

But I had no illusions about that. They might well be willing to hide us from the KGB or the police, but they could not take that decision without the permission of their superiors—the high priests of the Russian Orthodox Church—who, starting with Patriarch Alexei himself, had little love for me. I couldn't blame him. I had publicly expressed my contempt for that Church. It had never raised its voice against the crimes of Stalin. It had never championed the innocent, the dissidents, the millions who were shot, exiled, and imprisoned. The Church had prudently looked the other way, turned a deaf ear, swallowed its tongue. It had collaborated with a cruel and repressive regime. And even when times changed, even when *perestroika* and *glasnost* had finally made it possible to speak out without fear of reprisal, the Church had continued to play its despicable game, refusing to take a strong stand on anything that might really anger the government. I had said this and said it clearly during one of my television shows, and word had gotten back to me that Patriarch Alexei had been furious, had, in fact, made a few phone calls to see whether something might not be done to make me mend my irresponsible and impudent ways.

No, there was no sanctuary here—not for me, or, for that matter, for anyone the new government might be interested in getting its hands on.

There were no suspicious cars parked anywhere near my house. Nor were there any in my yard. I heaved a quiet sigh of relief.

Let me say that they never did come for me. Had the coup been successful, had they remained in office for more than three days, had they had the time to start dealing with those whom they considered risky, disloyal, unpatriotic—well, I have no doubts they would have dealt with me, along with a great many others who had become well known, whose careers had blossomed during the Gorbachev period, who for many stood as the symbols of change and progress. As for the apprehension I felt driving into my courtyard that morning, I must confess that feeling never left me until the coup failed. Every time I heard the rumble of a motor in our yard, every time I heard loud voices, I would step up to one of the windows —not smack to the middle, but over to the side—so that I could look out without being seen and check out the scene. Every night for three nights I went to bed with the expectation of being woken up at two or three in the morning by loud banging on our door and of seeing, through the glass peephole, three or four armed men in uniform standing there.

I suppose I was exaggerating my own importance. Also, the Emergency Committee had no intention of being perceived as anything but the legal heir of Gorbachev's *perestroika,* a group of civilized and democratic civil servants who had had an enormous responsibility thrust upon them by the untimely illness of their president and the country's national crisis. At least that was the impression they desired to create—for beginners. As for what might follow . . .

About one week before the coup, around August 12, the Pskov Automatic Telephone Station Producing Plant received an order to produce some two hundred fifty *thousand* pairs of handcuffs. According to the plant's deputy director, the order was placed by a man who represented a Moscow enterprise called Agro-converse and who offered to supply the plant with whatever amount of steel might be necessary to make the finished product. When the deputy director explained that he could not accept the order without the permission of the Ministry of the Interior, the man promised him that would not be a problem. Who were those handcuffs designated for? . . .

One of the first things I did when we entered our apartment was to open the mailbox for the papers. There was only one, *Pravda,* and it said absolutely nothing about the coup—proof that everything had been kept under wraps. But there was one article which I clipped and have kept ever since. Headed ''Who Is Insulting Whom?'' it was signed by Alexei Ilyin, one of the paper's deputy editors. I had recently interviewed Ilyin on my show, when we debated the role of the media in Soviet society, and he had come across as intelligent, well-spoken, and credible— very different in style from the author of this crude attack on one of the founding fathers of *perestroika,* Alexander Yakovlev. Just a few days prior to this article's appearance, Yakovlev had resigned from the Communist Party of the Soviet Union. Had Yakovlev not done that, he would have been expelled—the Party's Central Control Committee had, in fact, recommended just that. Now Ilyin was taking Yakovlev to task for what he had written in his resignation:

''In the resignation it is stated that the Central Control Committee's recommendation that he be expelled from the Party is a personal insult and a crass infringement on the basic rights of a Party member. While Yakovlev passes over his own statements and activities—the subject of the Central Control Committee's decision—he levels a series of accusations at those who criticized his political activities at plenary sessions of the Central Committee . . . as well as in the mass media. These accusations, according to Yakovlev, are not only baseless but assumed the proportions of a witch-hunt after the Twenty-eighth Congress, a witch-hunt organized and co-ordinated by the apparatus of the Central Committee of the CPSU (Communist Party of the Soviet Union). In his opinion, an influential Stalinist group has been formed at the heart of the Party leadership and it is in the process of casting off the Party's democratic wing, it is preparing its own comeback plans of social revenge, while scheming to take over the Party and engineer an anti-government coup. . . ."

Mr. Ilyin further wagged a strict finger at Yakovlev for his intolerance and continued: "As for his accusation concerning the preparation of a coup d'état, that not only flies in the face of Party ethics, but in fact of legal norms as well."

There was a painful kind of irony in this being published and appearing the very day of the coup that Yakovlev had so presciently predicted.

Television was still showing us *Swan Lake.* I turned on the radio. There was nothing but music. Moscow Echo, a radical and independent station that had acquired a large following in recent months, was nowhere to be found. *Swan Lake* faded away and was replaced by an announcer whom I had never seen before, a young lady who began to read "Decision Number One of the SCSE U.S.S.R."—a series of measures aimed "at protecting the vital interests of the peoples and citizens of the U.S.S.R., as well as the country's independence and territorial integrity, at reestablishing law and order, at stabilizing the situation, at overcoming this most terrible crisis, at avoiding chaos, anarchy, and fratricidal civil war." There were sixteen measures in all, number eight of which read: "Establish control over the mass media, that responsibility being given to a special body created within the SCSE USSR." So now I knew why Moscow Echo was not echoing. . . .

"Call Peter," Katherine said.

He was staying with a close friend of ours in Brooklyn. I dialed the number and got through immediately. It was about 2:30 A.M. in New York; Peter had been fast asleep. In his case that meant it would take cannon shots to wake him. It took me at least two or three minutes of intense talking to make him understand what my call was about. When I felt he was registering what I was saying, I told him his mother and I thought it would be better if he did not come back. "Wait a week or so. See what happens." Peter did not seem too responsive. "What about my visa?" he asked mildly. I told him I would call friends in Washington. They would, hopefully, understand the situation and take care of his visa. We let it go at that.

Katherine seemed to be very relieved. I somehow hoped Peter would ignore what I had said and come home, but I kept my hopes to myself.

I decided to take a little walk. I went out and approached Slava, one of the Patriarch's security men. "What's up?" I asked. Slava shrugged. "Nothing much. The Patriarch will be going out to celebrate." I looked at Slava. "Celebrate? Celebrate what?" Slava had just returned from a four-week vacation in southern Russia. His blond hair was bleached almost white by the sun, as were his bushy eyebrows. His skin was very pink, and his eyes were baby blue—all this making him look awfully innocent and, yes, cherubic. He smiled at me and said, "Didn't you know? Today is the Transfiguration of our Lord Jesus Christ."

The Transfiguration. Well, that certainly was an interesting coincidence.

I walked. Out to the Garden Ring, left to Kalininsky Prospect all the way down to the Alexander Garden running along the Kremlin wall, right toward Manezh Square. The tanks were everywhere. They reminded me of locusts, steel locusts that belch stinking fumes from their exhausts. They stood everywhere, the soldiers looking out of the turrets, their faces expressionless. At first there were not many people around, but gradually their number increased. Soon there were throngs everywhere. Some people taunted the soldiers, others clambered up on the tanks, stuck carnations and tulips into the gun muzzles. Yet others brought drink and food to the soldiers: "Would you shoot me? Would you shoot us?" "If I was ordered to." "Yes, if you were ordered to?" "No. Never." "Hey, wait a minute, an order is an order." "So you would shoot?" "I'm a serviceman, I took an oath to obey orders, to serve the country." "You think you serve your country by shooting me, asshole?"

The conversations swirled over Manezh Square like little tornadoes. Strangely enough, there were very few officers to be seen. Once in a while one would pop out of a tank or an armored vehicle, look around, and pop right back in. They certainly did not seem to like what they were seeing.

I walked. Up Tverskaya Street, renamed Gorky street in the thirties, now back to its original name. Armored cars and tanks were everywhere. There was a huge crowd in front of the red-and-white building of the Moscow City Council, the home of Moscow's radical leadership. The people stood there, milling around, waiting for something to happen. What?

It was a strange scene. Most Muscovites were acting as if nothing had changed. Shopping, going to work, whatever, looking neither right nor left, immune to the tanks and the soldiers all around them. How many years can you pretend nothing is going on? Lincoln was right: You can't fool all of the people all of the time. But that's not really necessary. What you can do is scare the living daylights out of them and create a generation or two of people who are born scared. They are easy to handle. It really doesn't matter what they think or believe. What matters is that they are scared. Can you scare all of the people all of the time? Or enough of them long enough that nothing else really matters?

I walked. Up Tverskaya, past Pushkin Square, up to Mayakovsky Square, then left on the Garden Ring and down to Vosstaniye Place, past the United States embassy . . .

What was the West going to say about all this, I wondered? And President Bush, what about him? I had become accustomed to the huge crowd that assembled Mondays through Fridays in front of the embassy, thousands of people applying to go to America—some to visit friends and relatives, others to go for good. Thousands of people, who for years and years had listened to the Voice of America encouraging them to defect, to come live in the land of the free and the home of the brave, now could not even get a tourist visa without being interviewed by some consular officer, often in the most insulting tones, almost always with a hint of suspicion that they were lying when they said they only wanted to visit a friend, that their real intention was to stay in America. It was President George Bush who had decided to curtail the flow of Soviet immigration. These people had been used for a political purpose, as we are all used by our governments, by our elected representatives in office. But now that there were no more dissidents, now that the Cold War was over, now that someone's defecting no longer was headline material, Soviets were no longer welcome.

I found myself thinking about that as I wondered what

George Bush would say about the coup. His attitude could be of major importance. Later I learned that Bush had indeed delivered a statement calling the coup an "extra-constitutional . . . disturbing development . . . that could have serious consequences." He also added that he thought it "also was important to note that coups can fail."

And that was all? For some insane reason it made me think of that wonderful scene in *Cyrano de Bergerac* when the Viscount de Valvert gropes for the strongest kind of invective to humiliate Cyrano and comes up with: "Monsieur, you have . . . a very big nose." And that is all? asks Cyrano, that is the best you can do? And he then delivers a scintillating and scathing tirade of what he would have said, had it been his choice.

George Bush is no Cyrano, to be sure. But was that really the best he could do?

A week or so after the coup I remember reading an interview with Marco Panella, a member of the European Parliament. When asked by a Soviet correspondent to give his assessment of the European Economic Community's and the Parliament's reaction to the coup in the Soviet Union, he said:

"It was quite traditional; nothing else should have been expected. At face value the reaction was faultless; in essence it was anti-democratic, cautious, not to say cowardly. What did you expect? For over half a century the Western democracies have cohabited with dictatorships, provided the latter did not show any aggressive intentions towards them. They did it with Mussolini, they did it with Hitler and Franco, later they did it with Stalin. . . ."

How true. They also did it with countless other dictators in Latin America, the Middle East, Africa, and Asia. They are still doing it today—China being just one example of that.

I had always argued that the leaders of the Western

world did not really care about how we in the Soviet
Union lived; nor did they care about the lives of any other
people anywhere in the world. It was all politics. As long
as they did not feel threatened, well, it was business as
usual. And now this wishy-washy statement coming from
the mouth of the "Leader of the Free World." "You have
. . . uh . . . a very big nose," he had said, and his allies
had joined in with similarly powerful indictments.

I walked. Back a little bit, then left, past the Moscow
Zoo, then left again and down toward the embankment of
the Moskva River and the grand stairway of the Russian
Parliament building. Tanks were clanking along with me,
more and more people getting in their way. Then a man
dashed out and blocked one of the tanks with his
body. The machine stopped and began to huff and puff,
while the man raised his arms and put both hands up
against the tank's front armor. "You're not going anywhere, hear me? You're not going anywhere!" he yelled,
hatred filling his voice.

The man looked to be about fifty. He was nearly bald
and obviously poor. He was wearing what had once been
a purple sweater—it looked almost colorless now—and a
pair of baggy, wrinkled trousers and sandals on his bare
feet. A net bag holding a few packs of Dimok cigarettes
dangled from one of his upraised hands. He stood there,
his face white—from the effort and from fear—eyes
closed, ignoring the militiaman who was asking him to
step aside. The militiaman was joined by a lieutenant colonel. Neither of them touched the man, nor even raised
their voices—the crowd standing there and sullenly
watching was no less threatening than a black thunder
cloud in the sky. The man opened his eyes, turned his
head to look at the two uniformed officers, and spat out:
"Back off . . . you jerks. This mother isn't going nowhere."

The tank belched a cloud of black smoke and lunged

forward, throwing the man back. The crowd drew a huge collective breath, but the man charged back, even whiter than before, clamped both hands on the tank's armor and yelled:

"You're still not going through! No way!"

"Get back." A young man was standing next to him, holding him by the forearm. "Get back."

A voice from the crowd: "Who the hell are you?"

"I'm from the KGB." The answer was like saying "and that is that." Only it wasn't.

"Get the fuck out of here!"—a roar from the crowd.

Suddenly I found myself thinking about how things had changed since the first time Soviet armor had come clanging into a Soviet city, since the Soviet armed forces had first been used to quell democracy in the Soviet Union . . .

Flashback: Tbilisi, the Dress Rehearsal

Georgia, an ancient, tiny land of plenty ringed by the Caucasus Mountains on the north and the Black Sea to the south, has always attracted the imagination of writers. According to Homer, this is where Jason sailed on his fabled *Argo* to take the Golden Fleece. In much more recent times, such Russian poets as Pushkin, Griboyedov, and Lermontov willingly fell under Georgia's spell and wrote about the land and its people with profound love and admiration.

According to one of many local stories, the land of Sakartvelo (that is what the Georgians call their country) was the result of a fortunate mistake. God was distributing pieces of land to the different nations he had created. He called the French and gave them France. He called the Greeks and gave them Greece. And thus he called them one and all, giving them their land. Finally, he finished. He heaved a sigh of contentment and was about to walk away, when suddenly he heard a puny voice calling, "What about us, God, what about us?" God looked down and saw the people of Sakartvelo. "Holy cow," thought God (or words to that effect), "I completely forgot about those people. If I don't give them something, they are going to make a terrible nuisance of themselves." So God said, "I was saving a piece of land all for myself, but I suppose I have no choice now but to give it to you. Here, take it and be quiet."

And that is how the land of Sakartvelo was born.

God was right in assessing the character of the people of Sakartvelo. They refuse to be quiet. They make a nuisance of themselves. They are fiercely independent. Throughout history they have refused to bow to any foreign potentate—no matter what. They fought the Tartars, the Arabs, the Turks, always against overwhelming odds. There were times when they came close to being annihilated, when it seemed their very language and culture would be destroyed. But somehow they survived and maintained their independence.

But in the early nineteenth century, threatened by Persia and the Ottoman Empire, Georgia accepted the least of all evils and agreed to come under imperial Russia—after all, it was a Christian eagle, and the Georgians were mostly Christians. Even so, the people of Georgia never surrendered their independence. Some day, they knew, they would be free. They preserved that fire in their hearts throughout the years of tsarism and throughout the Soviet period. Time and time again they made their passion known. So when Gorbachev took the lid off with *perestroika,* it was only a matter of time before Georgia began to boil over—and it was also only a matter of time before the opponents of *perestroika* saw this as an opportunity to act.

The student riots of November 1988 were the first hint of things to come. They were a response to Georgia's new constitution, imposed by Moscow, which in essence was discriminatory vis-a-vis the Georgian language. Several hundred students went on a hunger strike. This was followed by a series of rallies and meetings involving thousands of protestors. Things were on the verge of exploding when Gorbachev personally appealed to the people of Georgia and promised that all of their demands would be carefully considered before the final draft of the constitution was presented. The appeal was met with approval and joy in Georgia; the conflict was resolved. But four months later, when new demonstrations erupted, Gorbachev was not there to appeal for calm—he was on an official visit to the United Kingdom. One of the ranking officials accompanying him was Eduard Shevardnadze, the minister of foreign affairs and—coincidentally—a Georgian. Here is Shevardnadze's account of what happened:

"On April 7, late in the evening, the Soviet delegation headed by M. S. Gorbachev, and of which I was part, returned to Moscow after an official visit to Great Britain. As usual, we were met by officials at the airport. There, Mikhail Sergeyevich gave a thirty-minute briefing concerning the results of our negotiations in London. After that, as I recall, Nikolai Ivanovich Ryzhkov [then chairman of the Council of Ministers, the main executive body of the Soviet government] informed us concerning those parts of the country where strikes had created an extremely tense situation. There was also other information, including some related to Georgia. We were told about the mass demonstrations and that the local leadership had repeatedly asked for help in restoring order.

"We were also informed about a meeting held that morning at the Central Committee of the CPSU, at which all necessary measures had been adopted, including the sending of troops back from Armenia to Georgia, troops which usually were quartered in Tbilisi. . . . We were also told that the first deputy minister of defense and a deputy minister of the interior were already in Tbilisi. . . . During this briefing at the airport Gorbachev categorically demanded that, no matter what, the situation be resolved only by political means."

Shevardnadze, acting on Gorbachev's request, contacted the party leadership in Tbilisi. He was told that no additional aid was necessary. On the following morning, April 8, he received a telegram from Tbilisi, informing the Politburo that the situation was under control. "But in the early morning hours of April 9," continues Shevardnadze, "I received a call from Gorbachev: 'What has happened in Tbilisi? I have just been told a demonstration was dispersed, that people have been killed.' I told Gorbachev that I had just received the same information. I told him I would immediately try to find out what was going on. . . ."

Shevardnadze never did find out. Or, if he did, he never made it public. Immediately after the massacre he was sent to Tbilisi on a fact-finding mission. Nearly two years later, recalling that visit, Shevardnadze made the following statement:

"I expressed my personal view at a plenary session of the Central Committee of Georgia's Communist Party—that was on April 14 of last year. . . . I unequivocally condemned the punitive action against the demonstrators. . . . Let me repeat now what I said then: If there is no threat to anyone's life, health, or honor, if a meeting or a demonstration does not break the law, then one must deal with such events as the laws prescribe. This is all the more so when women and children make up a large part of a demonstration."

It is true that at the April 14, 1989, plenary session Shevardnadze condemned "the death of innocent people." But it is also true that he made the following statement:

"People talk about the peaceful character of the events which preceded the April 9 tragedy, but they say nothing about those calls that were far from peaceful, calls for blood that rang out on the eve of those events. Some people, who wish to be idolized by our youth, not only ignored their responsibility vis-a-vis the young people they pretend to lead, but in fact flouted their disrespect for the law, for order, for the Constitution.

"While not wishing to assume the role of prosecutor, I wish to say that I cannot overcome the feeling that some of the leaders of the so-called unofficial organizations deliberately led people who trusted them to their death."

That hardly jibes with any "unequivocal condemnation." I say this not because I wish to cast a shadow of doubt on Mr. Shevardnadze's integrity. Rather, I am trying to demonstrate how people whose integrity there is no reason to suspect were changed by radical events.

Exactly what did happen in those dawn hours of April 9, 1989? Basically, this:

Some ten thousand demonstrators were surrounded by tanks and armored cars and then attacked by armed military personnel wielding trench shovels—short spadelike shovels with sharp, triangular heads. People were hacked, stabbed, and gassed. Nineteen died, 167 were wounded. Those are the bare facts. But what do we know about their circumstances?

Anatoly Sobchak, the mayor of St. Petersburg, was in those days one of over two thousand People's Deputies who had been elected to the Supreme Soviet in what were the first-ever remotely democratic elections held in the history of the Soviet Union. An outspoken and brilliant law professor, he was appointed by Parliament to head an investigative commission concerning the Tbilisi massacre—and he personally handpicked the members of that commission. Nearly eight months later, Sobchak was ready to report. The sum total of the commission's findings were as follows:

• Although there were many mass meetings held prior to April 9, they were peaceful in nature. Not a single case of violence was registered or reported not only in Tbilisi, but in all of Georgia.

• The meetings were a natural expression of a normal democratic process, of the people's desire to be independent, to see Georgia once again become a sovereign state.

• The local leadership, especially the Party, did nothing to avoid the conflict. In fact, the republic's entire leadership stood at the windows in the Government House, overlooking the square, as their own people were being killed. And they did nothing at all, even though they had the authority to call off the troops.

• The military operation was headed by General Rodionov, commander of the Transcaucasian Military Zone. According to a directive, signed by General Moiseyev of the General Staff, the army was sent to "protect," to "preserve order," and to be used "as might be deemed necessary." The ambiguity of that last formula was what allowed the Georgian leadership to ask General Rodionov to use force —which he then did.

• In fact, the decision to send in the army was taken at a Politburo meeting held in Moscow on April 7 and presided over by Yegor Ligachev. President Gorbachev was not present, although Prime Minister Ryzhkov was. In point of fact, the Politburo did not have the legal right to call in the army. No Communist Party organization had that right—only the executive branch of the government did. The decision, hence, was illegal.

The Sobchak Commission also discovered that on the day before the tragic events, that is, April 8, the army was given the green light to intimidate the population of the Georgian capital. For that purpose three columns of armor and men, covered by low-flying attack choppers, marched through the city. Far from scaring the people—Georgians do not scare easily—this fed their wrath. The people also interpreted this piece of sabre-rattling as a prelude to the use of force against the two to three hundred demonstrators who stead-fastly had refused to leave the square in front of the Government House. Instead of staying away, people came to show their support—ten thousand of them crammed the square. It took General Rodionov a mere twenty-one minutes to clean them out: The army attacked scientifically, using both the trench shovels and a poison gas called CS. (Initially the military denied using either of these.) Then paratroopers were sent in to mop up—something personally prohibited by the minister of defense.

The Sobchak Commission made its findings public in September 1989. A few months later, during the February 1990 Plenum of the Central Committee, Yegor Ligachev, the same man who planted the infamous Nina Andreyeva article, the man who conducted the special Central Committee meeting where it was decided to send the army into Tbilisi, challenged the Sobchak Commission's findings and spoke about "an anti-Party, anti-Soviet plot" in the making. In reality, the plot was anti-*perestroika*. What happened in Tbilisi was not instigated: It had begun as a bona fide popular movement for democracy and independence. But it was soon perceived as being an opportunity to test the army.

The Sobchak Commission's findings were unequivocal: What had happened in Tbilisi was a crime, the army had been used against unarmed, defenseless people. This was in complete contradiction to the law. But *not one single person was punished for this.* On the contrary. General Rodionov received a promotion. . . .

Later speaking in Rodionov's defense, the minister of defense, Dmitri Yazov, said, "Sometimes unfortunate things happen even though they are done for a good and noble cause. . . . Rodionov is no greenhorn to have his butt kicked by whoever has that inclination. . . . General Rodionov commanded the army in Afghanistan for two years. I visited him there, and I know what a courageous and responsible person he is."

It must really have taken courage to send troops against unarmed people. . . .

While the Tbilisi events were making headlines, the military were quietly flexing their muscles in the Baltic cities of Riga, Tallinn, and Piarnu. . . . Very few people noticed that, but some did and brought the issue to Yazov's attention. His response was a study in duplicity: "These maneuvers are being conducted as part of a training exercise. They in no way are aimed at intimidating our comrades in the Baltic republics." He then paused and added: "Military vehicles sent to patrol the streets of those cities may have been a reaction to a demonstration that was held in front of the Baltic Military Zone headquarters in Riga."

The Sobchak Commission's findings were largely ignored. Instead, the office of the attorney general was asked to conduct an investigation. In early March of 1991, after months of hemming and hawing, the results of that investigation, signed by Attorney General Nikolai Trubin, were made public. Those results constituted a total whitewash of the army and the Party.

When the Tbilisi events were announced, most of us, myself included, had no idea what they really represented. We saw them as yet another tragic illustration of the Party's inability to deal with the current situation, as yet another example of misread signals. We could not have imagined that in fact Tbilisi was a dress rehearsal.

I walked. Past the Russian Parliament building where, one hour later, Boris Yeltsin would stand atop a tank and deliver his address "To the Citizens of Russia," calling on the nation to fight back, to go on strike. Was he grandstanding when he did that? Perhaps. But it was the best kind of grandstand move possible, because it brought hope. It told us all that at least there would be a fight, that if we died, we would die standing up, not on our knees. It spoke to our pride and to those things that had been taken away—to our sense of self-respect, to our identity.

I walked. Here and there people stood in groups reading photocopied leaflets of Boris Yeltsin's ukases. They seemed to be everywhere: on building walls, in the metro stations, even pasted onto the tanks and armored cars in the streets. In one, Yeltsin declared the Emergency Committee anti-constitutional, qualified its activities as a criminal coup d'état. He declared all decisions taken by the Emergency Committee unlawful and called on the population of Russia to disregard them. Anyone who accepted the orders of the Emergency Committee was breaking the law and would be prosecuted.

In another, Yeltsin declared the eight members of the Emergency Committee and all of their collaborators outlaws. He also appealed to one and all to act in accordance with the constitution and laws of the U.S.S.R. and the Russian Federation, guaranteeing all citizens, as president of Russia, legal protection and moral support. "The fate of Russia and the Union are in your hands," stated the ukase.

The ukases were read aloud as hundreds of people strained their necks to hear better. The police looked on with smiles on their faces and did nothing at all.

And what about Yeltsin? How come he was free to distribute his leaflets? Why had he not been arrested? According to some sources, he had been warned about the coup several hours before it began by loyal KGB officers. But that is not true. This was one of the rare instances when there were no leaks.

When I was driving into Moscow, Yeltsin was still out in the country, at his *dacha,* along with his closest associates Ivan Silayer, Ruslan Khazbulatov, Alexander Rutskoy, and Mikhail Poltoranin. He was joined there by

Anatoly Sobchak, the mayor of St. Petersburg, and Yuri Luzhkov, vice mayor of Moscow. Yeltsin and his group did not reach the Russian Parliament building until ten-thirty that morning.

Why, one must ask, were Yeltsin and his closest allies not arrested? Unbelievable as the answer may seem, it is true that the plotters were supremely confident of their power: Initially they did not perceive Yeltsin to be a threat.

It was about 2 P.M. when I got home. Katherine told me the phone had been ringing off the hook. The BBC, ABC, NBC, Australian TV, the CBC, and several other television companies had called. They all wanted an interview. I was expecting that.

The phone rang; it was one of the ABC bureau reporters. Would I be willing to go on *Nightline* to discuss the situation? I said I would have to think about it. I told him I needed more information, that I had to figure out exactly what I wanted to say. The ABC man was persistent: When would I be ready to give an answer? "Don't push me," I said, feeling anger beginning to take over, anger made greater by shame. "I'll tell you when I'm ready."

"That's fine," said the ABC man. Did I hear a touch of scorn in his voice?

The calls kept coming in, and I kept dodging them. I had a wonderful answer for them: I have to give serious thought as to whom I speak to—because, chances are, I may be able to speak only once; so I want to reach the largest possible audience, and I have got to figure out which program gives me the best shot.

That was all true enough. But underneath it lay the shame. If I kept my mouth shut, if I kept a low profile, if I gave the junta no special reason to come after me, then maybe things would blow over. I did have airplane tickets for Katherine and myself. We were scheduled to fly to New York on September 22; we even had our U.S. visas. Peter was in New York. Our daughter, Ekaterina, was in

Berlin with her husband and daughter. So we just might be able to quietly slip out—provided I did not start making a fuss on television. . . .

God, how I despised myself for those thoughts. How I hated myself for the fear I was again feeling. It sat there in my belly, cold and slimy, paralyzing me. I had thought it was gone forever. I had thought I had conquered it, broken away, that I was finally free. Now it was back, smirking at me, rubbing my face in my own vomit.

I sat there, letting the phone ring, hearing the answering machine record the voices, the endless chatter: "This is the BBC calling for Vladimir Pozner . . ." "Mr. Pozner, this is CBS . . ."

I don't know how long I sat there. I must have dozed off, because I was startled by Katherine's voice calling me upstairs to watch a telecast of the Emergency Committee's news conference.

What a sorry looking group, I thought, as I looked them over from left to right: Tizyakov, a man I had never seen before; Starodubtsev, the champion of "socialist farming"; Pugo with his fringe of dark hair and his rubber face; Vice President Yanayev; and Baklanov, the man behind the Soviet Union's military-industrial complex. As my father would have said, they all looked as though someone had shat in their soup.

Where are the others, I wondered, the big boys, Defense Minister Yazov, KGB chief Kryuchkov, Prime Minister Pavlov? Too busy with other matters? But then the news conference began—and it totally captured my attention. Not because anything of any importance was said, but because of what seemed like a preposterous takeoff on a real news conference. It was *Saturday Night Live* in Moscow. The impostors on the podium were exactly that: impostors. They did not believe a word they were saying. When Yanayev stated that Gorbachev was ill, the press hall, packed as it was to capacity, laughed out loud—and Yanayev smiled. When he referred to Gorbachev as "my friend," the journalists hooted—and Yanayev smiled. They all looked almost helpless, as if they had been dragged out here and forced to perform, like seals in a circus—but with much less pleasure.

Into the conference about twenty minutes, Yanayev's hands began to shake and his fingers began to tremble. Was it from drink? No matter. "Trembling fingers" jokes spread around the country with the speed of lightning.

There was really very little worthy of serious attention. I recall only Yanayev's denouncement of Yeltsin, saying the Russian president's call for a general strike was irresponsible; he also said that barricades were supposedly being built around the Russian Parliament building. If that is the case, said Yanayev, Boris Yeltsin bears all the responsibility for whatever consequences may follow.

While I was watching that news conference something rather important actually was going on. Valentin Pavlov had convened a meeting of the Cabinet at 6 P.M. to discuss the top government officials' attitudes toward the coup. No official notes were taken during that meeting, although in the following days several newspapers received "verbatim" reports of who had said what. The reports were subsequently denied by virtually all the ministers, which is not surprising, considering they were shown to have supported the coup. These were all typical Soviet elite apparatchiks, and there is really very little reason to believe they would have attempted to go against what they considered to be the dominant political current.

It is true that after the meeting Pavlov had to be whisked off to a hospital because of acute high blood pressure, but that probably had much less to do with political passions than with too much vodka and excitement. . . .

Something else important did happen while I was watching that news conference, something very important: It became clear to me that Mikhail Gorbachev had not been killed.

Even though the men on that stage had no qualms about distorting facts and would have said (did say) whatever suited their purposes—including lying about Gorbachev's being ill if he had been dead—there were too many signs confirming Gorbachev was indeed alive. It was not just Yanayev's absurd statement about "looking forward to working with my good friend Mikhail Sergeyevich in the near future"; nor was it the general singsong about Gorbachev's "simply being exhausted, nothing more serious"; nor, finally, was it Baklanov's amazing response to an after-conference question by a *Newsweek* correspondent. (She had asked about Gorbachev's health and he had shot back in exasperation, "He's fine, absolutely fine!"—thereby putting in question the entire justification for the change in leadership.) It was all of these things and something else, something more, something intangible and yet undeniable.

As I heaved a silent sigh of relief, I found myself thinking back to my pre-Gorbachev life, marveling at how that life had changed radically since Gorbachev's ascendance to the Soviet leadership. I found myself thinking about my own evolution from a person who had clung to the ideals of socialism and Communism, who had refused to give up on his convictions, who had refused to part with his illusions, and who had attempted to preserve them by rationalizing the realities of Soviet existence, to someone who had come to terms with himself and because of that was secure enough to accept reality as it was, rather than as what it might have been.

I thought back to all those years of living in the Soviet Union when I was considered suspect because of my past, my having been born and bred abroad, and also because I was the son of a French mother and, much worse, of a Russian-Jewish emigrant. I thought of how I had been denied entrance to Moscow University and how my father had had to fight to get me in; how I had been denied a meaningful job after having graduated. I thought about all those years when travel had been denied to me —even when my father was lying in a hospital in Dresden after a nearly fatal heart attack. I thought about how I had nearly always been able to reason with myself, find a justification for all of these, as well as for a myriad of other far more repulsive things.

I found myself wondering with a sense of repugnance at how I had denied myself the most prized treasure a human being is born with: open and independent thought.

I found myself remembering something my wife Katherine had shared with me only recently. It had to do with the endless and often passionate arguments that were waged in our kitchen between me and my closest friends, especially Yasha, a Leningrad physicist, and Zhenya, a Moscow artist. Both of them were always profoundly anti-Communist, and whenever we got together, which was often, we invariably became enmeshed in political debates which usually began calmly enough but had a tendency to become heated. There were even times when we traded insults. More often than not, when I felt I was becoming angry beyond control, I would look at my watch, get up, and say I was going to bed. Once, after I had stomped off to bed in a rage following a particularly acrimonious argument with Yasha, Katherine (who was never on my side) asked him to stop talking to me about politics. "Understand what you are doing," she told him, "you are trying to make Vladimir change his beliefs. If you succeed in destroying his ideals, you may lose a friend. He just might blow his brains out. Leave him alone."

Had I known about that conversation, I would have been furious. But Katherine was right. I had to come to whatever conclusions I might arrive at in my own good time. I could not be pushed without some sort of disastrous consequences. I needed time to prepare myself; I needed a certain sequence of events to push me in the right direction. Nothing could have been more perfect than what Gorbachev began.

To begin with, Gorbachev never bashed socialism nor its declared ideals. He bashed the malpractice of socialism in the U.S.S.R.—and that was precisely what I had always said and what I wanted to hear. In that sense, Gorbachev bolstered my views. Second, the changes in Soviet society under Gorbachev almost immediately and radically changed my life. Suddenly I was allowed to appear on Soviet television and address my fellow citizens, instead of being the "Made in U.S.S.R." product for export I had previously been. Suddenly I was being recognized by my fellow countrymen in my own country. I was able to participate in the general debate, actually even influence it, and feel that people appreciated what I was doing and supported me. Suddenly I was allowed to travel, to go back to New York City. But most important, I was allowed to speak my mind on whatever issue I wanted. And it was because of this last and most precious right that I myself began to change.

Do not ask me to explain how this happened, what kind of push-pull mechanism came into play, how my own freedom to speak affected—in fact, liberated—my mind. I would not know where to begin. But that is what happened. It was as if a tremendous load had been taken off my back, a load that had pressed me down, not really allowing me the luxury of raising my head. Now I could stand straight and face my own past and present. I suppose that is the way a Catholic feels after having spent time in a confessional, or the way one feels after having enjoyed a particularly productive session with one's analyst.

But while that analogy may be valid, it ignores one serious difference: The Catholic does not, as a result of having been confessed, start doubting the teachings of the Church; nor do most people rise from the analyst's couch with a decidedly less favorable view of psychoanalysis. The more Soviet society changed and the more I changed with it, the more critical I became of the man who was responsible for the change: Gorbachev.

This did not happen immediately, of course, but by the early spring of 1989 and especially because of the imperious and ill-mannered way Gorbachev treated Andrei Sakharov during the First Congress of People's Deputies, I began to take a much less accepting view of *perestroika*'s founding father. By the summer of 1990 I was more a Yeltsin man than a Gorbachev supporter. This is not to say that I had given up on the Soviet president, or that I no longer acknowledged the unique importance of his role for the twentieth century. Simply by casting away the dogma I had previously adhered to, I almost automatically began to see everything with a much more critical eye. As time passed and as it became more and more evident to me that Gorbachev was in the process of missing opportunities and that in his attempts to satisfy both the conservatives and the liberals he was beginning to look like Buridan's Ass, my support for this man began to wane and turn to anger.

Could Mikhail Gorbachev have done better than he did? Probably. Could someone else have done a better job? Maybe. Did he miss golden opportunities and thereby botch things? Yes, he did—and by so doing he let me down, he dashed my hopes (I prefer not to speak for others in so delicate a matter as this one, although I believe what is true for me is also true for many other people)—and that is what I could not and cannot forgive him for.

And so, as I quietly rejoiced at the knowledge that Gorbachev was alive, I simultaneously felt the rage in me boiling up, the desire to look him in the eye and ask: "You see what you have done?"

At the same time, I felt a great sadness for this man who had done so much, who had changed the world, but whose time was now up. And it really didn't matter whether he would remain president for a few months or even for a few years (although I very much doubted that would be the case). He had only one asset going for him: his weakness. Representing none of the republics, he could address them all without any one of them suspecting him of playing favorites. That role of strength through weakness could be played—but only for a while. As the republics became more and more rebellious, as the Soviet Union came apart—and nothing could stop it from doing so—Gorbachev's role would become more and more diminished. In a way, he reminded me of Churchill, the man who saved Britain in World War II and yet who was thrown out of office by what one would have thought to be a nation of ingrates. Gorbachev had freed the Soviet people—but there the similarity ended, because he had also blundered, refused to listen to reason, had played politics, and was responsible for what now seemed like a fatal blow to the democratic process he had engendered. The logic to Gorbachev's finale was tragic to be sure, but no less logical because of that.

Slightly later, during the evening news program, the new military commandant of Moscow, General-Colonel Kalinin, informed us that the state of emergency now applied to Moscow. This, he explained, was because of the activities of "irresponsible elements."

After the news, I turned to my wife and said, "I want you to understand something: I cannot stay silent. I have to speak out. I will despise myself and you will despise me for playing it safe. I know what you are thinking—will we ever see Peter again, will we ever be able to leave the country? If these men win, the answer is no. I have to fight back."

Katherine looked at me, smiled, and said, "Fight. Please fight. I was so hoping you would say that. Give them hell."

I folded her in my arms and we just stood there, hugging each other, holding onto each other as if the very world depended on it.

I went downstairs and called ABC. "I'll do it," I said. "I'll do whatever you can throw at me, *Nightline,* whatever. I'm your man."

When I hung up, I was feeling a joy as great as I had ever experienced. In this time of darkness, my spirits were soaring, my soul was singing. The fear was gone, conquered now I knew forever. Once again I pictured those men at the news conference. I thought about those eight leaders of the coup, all the president's men, each and every one of them appointed by Gorbachev. I kept thinking about how he had opted for them and, as I went to sleep, readying myself for tomorrow's battle, I kept thinking of what Gorbachev had done . . .

Flashback: "Companyyyyyy . . . Right!" The Scuttling of the "500 Days"

If there is one truth that is central to Marxist philosophy, it is that the root of all evil is private property. From ancient times, when the most coveted piece of property was the slave, to the modern, property, according to Marx, has bred greed, cruelty, egoism, inequity, war. Do away with private property, said Marx, and you create a new environment that permits human beings to truly realize their potential for good.

The above view was one that every single Soviet man, woman, and child was brought up on. It was the staple of films, children's stories, and plays; it was the subject of speeches, endless newspaper and magazine articles. It was discussed in virtually all textbooks, whether the subject was the alphabet or zoology.

Socialism's grand goal was to create a society based on property collectively owned by the people. Of all the different political and ideological views presented to the people of the Soviet Union, this one was, without question, the most widely shared. Along with that came the generally accepted outlook that being wealthy was somehow shameful— especially for a Soviet citizen.

It was okay to be, say, an American millionaire. After all, that was what America was about—making money, lots of it. Capitalists were *supposed* to be rich, weren't they? Not so Soviets. The revolution had been about getting rid of the rich, hadn't it?

The answer to that question is best answered by what I think is one of the greatest of all Soviet jokes. It involves an old countess, a descendant of one of the Decembrists,* who is sitting in her beautiful living room in St. Petersburg on November 7, 1917. She hears shots and shouts, so she sends out one of her maids to see what is happening. "What is all that noise about?" the old countess asks the maid when she comes back. "Revolution! The people are up in arms!" cries the maid. "Oh," says the countess, "and what do the people want?" "They want to do away with wealth." "How strange," muses the old countess, "my grandfather died because he wanted to do away with poverty."

While that story goes to the heart of what was wrong in the Soviet Union, it does not contradict the bias against wealth that sparked the revolution and burned strongly dur-

* A group of Russian noblemen who attempted to overthrow Tsar Nicholas I on December 14, 1825, and establish a democracy in Russia.

ing the following seven decades. One should not be surprised that Gorbachev's first and very tentative steps toward
a market economy were met with suspicion by the population at large. Those first steps allowed for the existence of
small private businesses: cooperatives and joint ventures.
Co-ops were, at least on paper, businesses jointly owned by
a family or a small group of individuals. Very importantly,
they were supposed to split all profits *equally*. Joint ventures
were presented as a way to attract foreign capital invest-
ment while keeping foreigners under Soviet control.

These businesses were presented as beneficial to all the
Soviet people. Supposedly they would lead to the opening
of cafés and restaurants, car repair shops and stores. They
would bring about the birth of a new and oh-so-needed
services industry, while the joint ventures would create market opportunities for the West, and lead to an influx of consumer goods.

None of this ever happened. On the contrary, from day
one the Party and government bureaucracy adopted measures that would either force the co-ops out of business or
put them into a situation where they would appear grasping
and greedy. The image of the co-ops would become so tar-
nished as to compromise their existence.

One of the adopted measures increased the price of anything procured by a co-op from a state outlet by a factor of
six. Thus, if a cooperative restaurant bought meat from a
state outlet, it had to pay six times as much for it as a state-
owned restaurant. That forced the co-ops to raise their
prices so high that the majority of Soviet citizens could not
afford them. Local government officials allowed co-ops to
sell whatever they produced at prices higher—even much
higher—than those of government-owned facilities, *but prohibited the sale of anything below government prices, even
when co-ops were prepared to do so.* A special tax rate was
devised to make the co-ops pay more—which forced them
to jack their prices up even higher. The average Soviet citi-

zen knew little, if anything, about the behind-the-scenes activities; what he did know was that he could not afford the co-op prices, that he was being ripped off. This hardly led to broad popular support for this *perestroika* invention. But that was not all.

Soon after the first co-ops opened, rumors began to circulate concerning the fact that most of the "cooperators" came from something referred to in the Soviet Union as the "shadow economy," that is, from the world of wheelers and dealers, profiteers and speculators who, during the Brezhnev years, had spun a web of corruption that enveloped the entire country at all levels. I will never forget the discussion I had with one co-op owner, who was probably the first to open a privately owned restaurant in Moscow (one that became spectacularly successful). I prefer not to give his name for reasons that the reader will appreciate as he or she reads on.

I recall telling this co-op owner, somewhat loftily, that he should not be surprised at the hostility people had toward co-ops, considering their owners' origins. He looked me in the eye and asked, in turn, "Did you open a co-op?" I said that I hadn't. "Would you?" he went on. I shook my head. "Of course not!" he spat out. "You are too noble, too frigging intellectual, you have a sense of fair play, of right and wrong and all that crap!

"Well, let me tell you something," he went on. "The only people who have the intelligence, the balls, and the hunger to go out there and fight this frigging system is us, we guys who were forced into becoming criminals because your fucking Communist Party officials stood around with their pockets wide open waiting for us to make them rich. Yes, we were the shadow economy, but, damn it, whose shadow were we? Who did I have to pay off to start working as a waiter in the Metropol Hotel? The maître d', that's who. And when I was promoted to maître d', the waiters payed me off, and I payed off the restaurant director. And when I became the restaurant director, I had to pay off the Party secretary of the fucking district because without his okay I could not get that job. And I don't mean I payed once. I payed twice a month, I goddam supported him and his family. Where the hell were you and all of your honorable intellectual buddies? Shit, you were giving us handsome tips in the Metropol while we were serving you only two thirds of everything you ordered, caviar included, and putting the difference in our pockets. So don't ask me about that shadow economy shit, okay?

"Ask about what's changed. I'll tell you that now we can work out in the open, now you come to my restaurant and nobody steals, you get the food you payed for, and it's good food, cooked with fresh butter, not stuff used over and over again. And the waiters are polite, and the service is quick, and the table cloth is starched and clean, and the lights are soft, and everybody smiles at you—that's what has changed.

"And you know what hasn't changed? I'll tell you what: I still have to bribe the fucking officials—otherwise I won't get the permission to open my restaurant."

He was right on target. Despite any idealistic rhetoric, the system remained corrupt. But, once again, the citizenry knew little about all that. And when many co-op restaurants and cafés decided to refuse to accept rubles in payment and began to take real money—that is, dollars, marks, francs, pounds, when only foreigners or Soviets with hard currency could enjoy the nice service and fine food—it led to more animosity from the people.

As for the joint ventures, they, too, were hobbled by all kinds of rules and regulations hindering their capacity to make a difference—so they made none. Meanwhile, the opponents of market economy and of Western participation quietly spread rumors about Russia's being "auctioned off to foreigners." The rigidly ideological mindset and the performance of the co-ops and the joint ventures became a

serious obstacle to rallying public opinion behind the idea
of developing a market economy in the Soviet Union.

Nevertheless, Gorbachev and most of his economic advisers were of the opinion that there was no other way to get
the country moving. They were careful not to use such ex-
pressions as "capitalism" or "private property," but they did
speak long and loud about "radical economic reform"—a
euphemism for both of these. Slowly, painfully, the process
moved forward. By the late summer of 1990 it finally began
to look as if Gorbachev was ready to make his big economic
move. By September he had publicly endorsed something
called the 500 Days plan, a bold, if imperfect, economic
blueprint developed by Stanislav Shatalin, a brilliant maverick of an economist, a member of the Academy of Sciences
of the U.S.S.R. and a member of Gorbachev's Presidential
Council. Shatalin developed the plan in collaboration with
Gregory Yavslinsky, an economist in his early thirties, someone who was virtually unknown except to experts in the
field, but who would become one of the most controversial
of the *perestroika* thinkers.

The 500 Days plan was devised as a means by which to
ease the transition from the previous command economy to
a market economy. It met with ferocious opposition. Some
of that opposition was ideological, gut level—it came from
the indoctrination of which I spoke earlier. Most of it came
from the bureaucracy which realized only too well that a
market economy meant relinquishing control. It meant no
longer having the power to grant or not to grant loans, to
sign or not to sign requests for spare parts, raw material,
government subsidies, increasing or lowering production
quotas. In short, it meant no longer being in charge.

And so, the bureaucrats fought back. What they did was
what they always had done when they could not completely
trash a new proposal: They proposed a plan of their own for
"radically reforming the economy," something called The
Government Version. This version was signed by none other

than Nikolai Ryzhkov, chairman of the Council of Ministers of the U.S.S.R. Thus, by summer's end, the two plans had emerged as the main contenders for where the country would go. Everything now depended on Gorbachev.

Addressing a group of Soviet and foreign newspaper correspondents on September 1, 1990, Gorbachev did his usual thing, a very effective routine that left people thinking, "Gee, that was great, but what did he actually say?" Only a careful reading of his speech, a careful cleaning away of excess tissue, allows one to understand that the president said quite a few important things. What it boiled down to was the following:

There are two plans to choose from and that is good, not bad, as the press would have us believe. Pluralism means choice, that is what we want. Alternative plans are a normal part of the democratic process; the press should draw neither horrified breath, nor, even worse, horrified conclusions.

The president should be granted emergency powers. That could entail a change in the structure and activity of the government. Incompetence and/or personnel inefficiency must not be tolerated, especially considering the present situation. Our approach should be balanced and responsible.

The Shatalin plan is good on several counts. It takes into detailed consideration the concrete conditions of the country, of each republic. It shares certain things with the Government plan, but there are also some serious differences. They include price reform, stabilization measures, taxes and tax policy, the budget, hard currency policy, to name some. (Those, according to Gorbachev, were the "main" areas of contention; one would like to ask, what did the two plans have in common?)

Once both plans have been analyzed, all the republics will be offered one grand scheme, a synthesis to satisfy all parties.

What Gorbachev was proposing was purely and simply

preposterous. The differences between the 500 Days plan and Ryzhkov's model were incompatible. But Gorbachev was Gorbachev. He had always played the game of marriage-maker, broker, king of the grand compromise. And he said nothing about the real issue, namely: Who would be calling the economic shots, Moscow, or the republics? The Shatalin plan was built around the view that, since all the republics had declared their sovereignty, they would decide their own economic matters.

In mid-September the Supreme Soviet was slated to endorse one of three plans—Shatalin's, Ryzhkov's, or what had come to be known as the Presidential plan, a synthesis of the two others. Addressing the Supreme Soviet on September 16, Shatalin once again explained that his 500 Days plan was only a first step toward a market economy, it did not presume to cover the entire process from A to Z. Shatalin then made a crucially important statement: "The country cannot afford to support a huge military establishment, especially considering that no one is threatening us; neither can we afford to support the huge KGB apparatus for which there exists no justification. Without reforming the budget and slashing defense and KGB-related expenditures, we cannot hope to move toward a market economy."

The army, the military-industrial complex, the KGB—all of them—saw the writing on the wall.

So where did Gorbachev stand in all of this? Addressing that same assembly two days later, the president did his best to placate those who might have suspected him of "going capitalist":

"Let us ask ourselves whether the standard of living we presently enjoy corresponds to the ideal of socialism? What about the alienation of the working man from his work, his not being able to participate in management—is that a feature of socialism? What about his security, his incentives, the degree to which he is involved in enjoying the fruits of his labor? Are we even close to socialism in all of these things?

"A second point. The market democratizes economic relations, and socialism is unimaginable without democracy. . . .

"Third. Only a balanced market can guarantee socialism's basic principle—compensation according to work. . . .

"Finally fourth—social security. The market economy allows for a qualitative improvement of that, enriching it with a truly socialist content."

In the vernacular, Gorbachev was telling the party bureaucracy, "Hey, guys, I'm for socialism." But he went much further. He rebuffed those critics of the Shatalin plan who called it a disguised road to capitalism. He said the private sector, as envisaged in this plan, would play an important role only in certain areas, while being very limited in general. He called for a referendum on whether or not land should be privatized.

At that point, September 18, 1990, Gorbachev was still on the Left, still for the 500 Days plan.

This infuriated not a few people, among them Vassily Starodubtsev, who took the floor to speak for what he called "all the peasants of the U.S.S.R." Starodubtsev trashed the Shatalin plan. He called privatization of the land "a step back" and added, "Why does the plan not contain a single word about socialism, about socialist orientation? Isn't that a retreat from the ideas of socialism and its values?" Starodubtsev then warned that, should Shatalin's program be adopted, he would immediately call an extraordinary convention of the Peasant League of the U.S.S.R., which he headed, and for a peasant strike. The message was clear: Go with Shatalin and we will starve the country.

Not surprisingly, Starodubtsev would become one of the eight members of the State Committee for the State of Emergency, or, in more recognizable terms, the junta.

On September 19, 1990, at a session of the Russian Federation's Supreme Soviet chaired by Boris Yeltsin, an overwhelming majority of the deputies supported a motion calling for the Ryzhkov government to resign. The vote was 164 to 1 with 16 abstentions. The session then adopted a resolution stating, among other things, that "the RSFSR [Russian Soviet Federative Socialist Republic] Supreme Soviet has concluded that the government of the U.S.S.R. is not capable of leading the country out of this profound economic crisis; is not capable of fulfilling its constitutional duties to protect the sovereignty of the RSFSR; it has lost the trust of the RSFSR Supreme Soviet; does not enjoy the support of the broad masses."

In my opinion, that resolution was what convinced Gorbachev. That was when he seriously considered turning his back not only on the liberals, on the democrats, on the radicals, but, most importantly, on the centrists whose mainstay he had been. Gorbachev began to move to the right.

Over the following few days it became clearer and clearer that Gorbachev was backing away from the 500 Days plan, as well as from the Ryzhkov plan, which he really never supported. He was now speaking up for the third plan, his plan, which, he insisted, included the best of both worlds. In effect that stymied any and all attempts by the republics to implement the 500 Days plan. Russia had announced it would start the 500 Days count on October 1. Now Stepan Silayev, Russia's prime minister, went on television to announce that the date had been moved back one month, to November 1, by which time he hoped the plan would be endorsed by the U.S.S.R.'s Supreme Soviet. Mr. Silayev was engaging in a bit of wishful thinking

On September 24, things came to a head. The president's personal adviser on economic policy, Nikolai Petrakov, told the Supreme Soviet that the Ryzhkov plan was merely a revamped version of a concept that Parliament had scrapped much earlier. It called for a huge price hike, scheduled for the first of the year, which supposedly would be *fully compensated.* "We are talking about a price hike totalling 135 billion rubles," said Petrakov. "Where is that money going to come from to compensate the consumer? The answer is simple: The government will print more money, paper money that has absolutely no meaning since there is nothing to buy."

Stanislav Shatalin: "The government plan talks about the market but uses that word to camouflage the old command economy system. . . . Its authors wish to ignore economic laws, which is just as realistic as trying to ignore dawn and dusk. Our plan envisages a new political and economic organization of our Union. The government view differs—and I find that view completely unacceptable."

In fact, the debate was far less about economic principles than about control and power. And that was the consideration underlying Gorbachev's decision to ditch the Shatalin plan.

On the morning of September 24, Anatoly Lukyanov announced an unplanned-for break in the session's work. During that time Gorbachev met with Shatalin, Ryzhkov, Lukyanov, and a few other very close advisers. After the break, Gorbachev came back with what he called the final draft of the plan which, he said, was a synthesis of the best ideas for radical economic reform. A last-ditch effort by the proponents of a market economy notwithstanding, Gorbachev's proposal passed. It included, among many other things, the granting of extraordinary powers to the president.

That setback for the democratic movement and reform in the Soviet Union was the most visible of a series of events, including one that was brought up during the afternoon session by deputy Belozertsev. Would Defense Minister Dmitri Yazov and KGB chairman Vladimir Kryuchkov please explain, he asked, why four airborne divisions and two paratroop brigades had been brought into Moscow? Would they also explain why two other airborne divisions had been transferred from the armed forces to the KGB? Also, why were the paratroopers wearing bulletproof vests, why were they armed, and what were they doing carrying cannisters of poison gas?

Kryuchkov said he would be happy to satisfy Belozert-sev's curiosity. He acknowledged that the Vitebsk Airborne Division had been transferred to the KGB. Several months ago, he said, when not all was calm in some frontier regions, this division had been incorporated into the KGB's Frontier Forces. That division had now been moved to Moscow only to participate in harvesting the crops. As for other troop movements, counterintelligence reports made it clear that there was nothing to worry about.

But in fact, there was a lot to worry about. This was a show of strength; it was a warning to Gorbachev to shape up. It was also a signal to all the hard-liners, telling them the time had come to strike back.

By the beginning of October, it had become evident that the 500 Days program was dead and buried and that the president had been granted the additional powers he desired by a conservative majority that expected him to do its bidding.

October was the start of a vicious smear campaign against Gorbachev's closest allies, specifically those who the right wing considered to be especially dangerous because of their influence and/or position: Alexander Yakovlev, Eduard Shevardnadze, and Minister of the Interior Vadim Bakatin. On October 4, Bakatin was forced to defend himself at a special hearing of the Presidium of the Council of Ministers, where he was accused of being "soft on crime."

At that same hearing Vladimir Kryuchkov, as head of the KGB, furnished a detailed description of how his organization was fighting organized crime—and scoring major successes (in contrast to what the police had managed to do under Bakatin's leadership). In 1989 and the first six months of 1990, said Kryuchkov, the KGB had terminated the activities of 1,200 organized crime groups and had recovered some 214 million rubles in money and valuables. Having thus demonstrated the KGB's efficiency as the nation's top crime fighter, Kryuchkov made his move: To successfully combat organized crime, he said, the KGB must legally be charged with that duty. Laws had to be passed specifying the concrete status of the KGB and the police. The KGB chairman also proposed that some of the money recovered from organized crime be used to create a special fund for the KGB and the police. Last, but certainly not least, he proposed that *the entire population of the U.S.S.R. be fingerprinted.* This, he said, would not insult honest, law-abiding citizens, but would serve the purpose of apprehending criminals.

The swing to the right had begun, but Gorbachev was still being pushed. Soon, he would start moving on his own. . . .

TUESDAY, AUGUST 20, 1991

It's raining. It started on the nineteenth and hasn't stopped since. Is that a sign?

There were only two papers in my mailbox this morning, *Pravda* and *Izvestia.* All the other periodicals I receive have been shut down—"temporarily," according to the coupsters, but nobody will be fooled by that statement.

There is really nothing to read in the papers, except the official statements issued by the Emergency Committee and "reports" describing how people here and abroad are reacting to the changes. The message is that, by and large, people here support the state of emergency, while abroad there is concern, but very little more. Some world leaders have come out in favor of these measures—Saddam Hussein, to name one, and Muammar Qaddafi, to name another. Interestingly enough, Fidel Castro seems to be hedging his bets. At any rate, there is no news about his support.

Television is a marvelous study in blandness: "Don't worry, be happy." The chairman of the State Television and Radio Broadcasting Company, Leonid Kravchenko, must be a happy man, I thought. This is what he was hoping for. In fact, this is what he had predicted many months ago. It had happened during a regular Monday morning meeting with the heads of departments and top commentators, when a barrage of criticism had been directed at the way State TV was turning right under Kravchenko. He had listened to all this, then said, closing the meeting: "You can criticize me all you want, but the day will come when you will understand how democratic a person I really am. Wait till I am replaced by a man with a gun."

While Kravchenko was not the man with the gun, he was very close to that. He was entrusted with the mission of breaking the news to the nation. On August 19, at 1 A.M., he was at the Central Committee headquarters. It was from there and at that time that he phoned Gennadi Shishkin, first deputy chief of Tass, the official Soviet wire service, and asked him to come over immediately. That was a serious break in tradition, because Tass had always been the number-one source of official information in the Soviet Union; as a matter of fact, no periodical, no TV or radio station was allowed to announce any news item of any importance if it had not been first announced, or vetted, by Tass. So why the change? There could be only one reason: Kravchenko was the most trusted. He not only would obey orders (as would most ranking Soviet officials—that was second nature to them), he would obey them to the best of his abilities for the pure and simple reason that he was by conviction a supporter of the hard-liners.

No, there was nothing to watch on television.

But radio was different. During the night of August 19 and the early hours of the twentieth, technicians had set up a studio for Radio Russia. It was a by-the-seat-of-your-pants operation. The signal did not carry very far; in fact, it did not even cover all of Moscow. But at least it was something. The service started at about 2 A.M. on August 20 and continued round the clock. Perched on the very top of the Russian Parliament building, the studio offered its animators a terrific view of the streets and avenues below. Whenever anything moved, whenever armored cars or tanks or military units appeared or pulled out, the journalists immediately informed their audience about this.

But Radio Russia did more than that. It brought hope because of the voices it carried. Voices of people known to one and all, writers and actors, politicians and military men, all of them sending a signal: Stand up for your freedom, we are here, we are with you. Come to the White House of Russia, come help build the barricades, come one and all, but come especially if you have done service in the armed forces. If you are a young man, this is the chance you do not want to miss, this is when you can serve Russia.

Perhaps the most electrifying voice of all was that of Rostropovich. Here was this genius of the cello, this incomparable musician who had been so terribly wronged by the Soviet government, who had been allowed to go on an international tour and who then had learned that his citizenship had been revoked and that he and his wife had been banished from their own country. Here was a man who had everything one might aspire to: fame, wealth, worldwide respect. He could have looked on what was happening in Russia from his comfortable home afar and made whatever statements he wished to make. Yet he had done something so profoundly different.

Rostropovich had, as he said, "put his things in order"

—meaning his will—and then, without telling his wife or anyone else, he had hopped on a plane and flown to Moscow.

He had acted as only a truly free person could act.

Every time I think of freedom, I am reminded of a story I have written about before and, probably, will write about in the future. It concerns a French Resistance fighter during World War II and the occupation of France. (The man was actually a Spaniard who had fought Franco in the Spanish civil war, then had fled to France, where the French had interned him in a special camp for all "leftists"—a page of history that the Western democracies have conveniently forgotten.) This Spaniard rose to become one of the leaders of the Resistance movement and, consequently, one of the most prominent people on the German "most wanted" list. Finally, he was apprehended and put in a solitary confinement Gestapo cell, where he was watched around the clock by armed guards.

One day a guard, more curious than most, asked this prisoner why he was in this jail, what was his crime. "I am here because I am a free man," answered the Spaniard. The German guard laughed. *"You* are in prison. *I* am the free man," he said. "You don't understand," answered the Spaniard. "I did not *have* to fight you. I could have stayed home, read the papers and sipped my wine. I did not have to risk my skin. But as a free man I had no choice. I had to fight you, because everything you stand for is against freedom. Had I not done that, I would have forfeited my freedom. As for you, you were ordered to put on a uniform, pick up a rifle and invade another country. No, you are not free. I am—and that is why you are on that side of the door and I am on this side."

Rostropovich acted as a free man. There is nothing more beautiful, more noble, nothing that so pumps up one's pride in being a human being than to be a witness to the actions of free men.

In addition to Radio Russia, Moscow Echo was back on the air. On the morning of August 19, when its editor Sergei Korzun opened the broadcast, he had had no choice but to read the statements of the Emergency Committee. He was waiting for some guests, mostly deputies of Russia's Parliament, to appear so as to begin the program in earnest. Guests did appear—that was at about twenty to eight—but not the ones he was expecting. They were from the KGB and they very politely asked Korzun to tell his listeners that Moscow Echo was going off the air due to technical problems. Korzun demanded he be shown a piece of paper authorizing the closing of his station—then, since none was produced, he refused to end the broadcast.

Meanwhile Yuri Shchekochikhin, an outspoken journalist and a member of the Russian Parliament, made his appearance. One of the two KGB officers had disappeared, the other continued to insist that the program be ended. Korzun asked Shchekochikhin to take the mike, but at that point one of the technicians came charging in to announce that the station was no longer on the air. They had been cut off—the other KGB officer had managed to force the technical department to pull the plug on the station.

Moscow Echo came back on the air at about twenty to two in the afternoon on the nineteenth, thanks to the support of a ranking official in the U.S.S.R. Ministry of Communications. That night, on *Vremya,* the television evening news program, Moscow Echo was attacked for "instigating disobedience" and spreading "provocative rumors"; it was officially banned. At ten minutes to eleven its transmitters were pulled.

Amazingly, Korzun managed to get back on the air at half past midnight on the twentieth (that was when I caught them; the rest of the story was put together later), but at exactly 1:19 A.M. Moscow Echo was cut off again. With President Yeltsin and the Russian Ministry of Communications putting on the pressure, the station was broadcasting again at 3:37 A.M. They had to work out of a cubicle the size of a toilet stall. There was room for one person who had to hold the mike—there was no room for a table or even a chair.

Moscow Echo stayed on the air until eighteen minutes past ten in the morning of the following day when a group of parachutists, headed by one Lieutenant-Colonel Zakharov, stormed the building where the transmitter was located and trashed it. But at 2:40 P.M. Moscow Echo was back on the air. From that point on it did not go off— except for a very short break because of a technical problem. Korzun and company worked for seventy-two hours nonstop. The technology had to take a break, it could not maintain the pace of free men, of men who refused to be intimidated, who refused to accept the idea of fear being a rationale for their behavior.

That was something the plotters had really never taken into consideration. First, because fear had always been part of their rationale, and they could not imagine its not affecting everyone else; second, because in the past fear had always worked, including the very recent past, applying to none other than Gorbachev himself. . . .

Flashback: Shotgun on Red Square

On November 7, 1990, during a parade on Red Square, a man pulled a shotgun out of his trousers, aimed at the distant figure of Gorbachev standing on the Mausoleum—but before he could pull the trigger, his arm was knocked up and the shot went sky high. The would-be assassin was immediately overpowered, flung to the cobblestoned ground, handcuffed, thrown into a car, and driven away.

Very few people even noticed the event, but that night both TV and radio reported it, as did the press the following morning. The story was not front-page news—it was played down rather than up. That is, it was given just enough prominence to reach everyone, but was not sensationalized—a clever move, since that would have made people suspicious.

Over the nearly forty years of my life in Moscow, I have only twice marched in a parade across Red Square: once, in 1955, when I was a student at Moscow University, and again in 1980 or '81, when I was working for Gosteleradio. In both cases, the occasion was November 7, the anniversary of the 1917 socialist revolution. For the reader's benefit let me explain the ritual: First, there is a military parade, then a parade of people who represent different organizations— for instance, Moscow University. Finally, these groups are followed by a parade of ordinary Muscovites. That is the way it once actually was. During Stalin's time the demonstration was the most interesting part of the event. Hundreds of thousands of Muscovites celebrated their revolution—endless waves of humanity rolled through Red Square dancing, singing, waving to their leaders who stood on the Lenin Mausoleum. The demonstration was spontaneous and lasted many hours.

Gradually that changed, although it was still true when I first proudly strode across Red Square. Perhaps there was not quite the same enthusiasm—after all, Stalin was no longer there. But I recall the excitement, the joy. I also recall how few people in uniform watched over us as we marched along, how easy it was for anyone to join the ranks of the marchers as they approached Red Square.

But by 1980 everything had changed. There was no more spontaneous demonstration. After the military parade came the civilian parade, rank after rank. Like the military, the civilians had been carefully selected at their place of work by the Party organization. They were checked out, then called into a meeting and told how to walk—not to straggle behind, not to stop in Red Square under any circumstances, not to allow anyone to join them when they assembled at their meeting place and walked through the streets toward their final destination. The closer one got to Red Square, the greater was the number of military and plainclothesmen. On the square there were literally hundreds of them watching the marchers' every move. They were protecting the leadership from . . . what? An assassin's bullet? That seems highly unlikely, considering how difficult it would have been to get a shot off. But the idea of danger was very much part of the siege mentality, which had, on the one hand, a certain justification in the Soviet Union's early history but, on the other, had been carefully nurtured by the KGB: The greater the threat to the system and its leaders, the more the KGB was necessary.

There is ample reason to believe that such KGB heads as Yezhov, Beria, and some others invented plots and then apprehended the "plotters" so as to not only gain and preserve the esteem and the gratitude of The Boss, i.e. the general secretary of the Party, but also to prove to him the necessity of that organization's existence and the need for its ever-growing power.

It is not inconceivable that the KGB leadership decided to capitalize on such previously unheard of things as strikes, rallies, political protest meetings, and even armed conflict in the republics. One of the best and most tested ways of making the leader see things in a desired light was to scare him into believing he was threatened. Thus, if Gorbachev could be persuaded to believe that the "radicals" were not above dumping him, that there were extremists ready to kill him, then he would be far more willing to cast his lot with the Right. The incident on Red Square certainly suited that scenario.

Did Gorbachev actually believe this was a planned assassination attempt? Who knows? But the fact is that November saw him really begin to change his tune. This became most apparent during the fourth session of the Supreme Soviet when, on November 11, Anatoly Lukyanov informed the deputies of a presidential decree relieving Vadim Bakatin of his duties as minister of the interior (chief of police) and replacing him with Boris Pugo. Bakatin the moderate was replaced by a hard-liner—and Gorbachev was immediately called on by the deputies to explain what this was all about. Gorbachev came back with a marvelous piece of hypocrisy. Bakatin was, in his opinion, more suited for political activity. Having arrived at that conclusion, said the president, he had decided more use should be made of comrade Bakatin's penchant for political maneuvering; a penchant that—"Let's admit it," emphasized Gorbachev—sometimes affected the organization he had been appointed to head, an organization that called for certain specific traits of character.

While many of the deputies were more or less willing to let that explanation pass, they balked at Gorbachev's appointment of army General Gromov as Pugo's first deputy chief of police. Pugo was certainly a hard-liner, but compared to Gromov, a man who had made a name for himself in Afghanistan, Pugo was a cutie-pie. The protests were loud and clear—and they were completely hopeless. Gorbachev had made up his mind. . . . Or, better said, he had been helped to make up his mind.

On November 2, in the Kremlin, Gorbachev received a group of seven deputies. All of them belonged to a parliamentary faction called Soyuz, which consisted of some seven hundred of the most hard-line communists. Among the most outspoken were two colonels, Alksnis and Petrushenko, and one Yevgenny Kogan who, as he put it, represented "the Russian-speaking people of Estonia." These three were among those who managed to secure an appointment with Gorbachev in the presence of Prime Minister Ryzhkov and the chairman of the Supreme Soviet's Presidium, Lukyanov. As we shall see, this meeting turned out to be extremely important.

But first let us ask ourselves: How did the Soyuz deputies manage to get to Gorbachev? Why were they accorded preferential treatment? The answer lies in the fact that only one person in the entire power structure could open Gorbachev's door—only one person could schedule a meeting with the president. That person was the president's chief of staff, Valery Boldin, a man who enjoyed the president's full trust. And also a man who agreed to help the junta take power . . .

Several months later, in the right-wing *Rabochaya Tribuna,* Kogan and Petrushenko went public concerning their discussion with Gorbachev.

Kogan: "We did not bandy words. We informed Mikhail Sergeyevich that if he did not take more conclusive measures, we would consider that as being sufficient reason for us to call for a no-confidence vote in Parliament."

Petrushenko: "Before leaving, we again demanded that Bakatin resign. We even told Ryzhkov that the Soyuz faction had not spoken out against his government, but that we would be forced to do so if Bakatin were to remain minister of the interior."

This was blackmail, pure and simple, this was an ultimatum. One should ask: Why didn't the president throw them out? Why didn't he make public what they had said? Was he afraid of them, or, more precisely, was he afraid of those who backed them? If that was the case (and it certainly seems to be), then Eduard Shevardnadze's resignation of December 20 takes on a special meaning, as do his words "I believe this calls for serious thought: Who backs these comrades, what are they really about?" Two days after Shevardnadze's resignation, the nominal head of the Soyuz faction,

Blokhin, stated, "We talked about Bakatin with the president."

That was the story behind the story of Bakatin's resignation. It had nothing to do with his so-called penchant for political activity. It had to do with politics, with the fact that the right wing wanted him out of office and was able to push Gorbachev hard enough to make him cry "Uncle!"

On November 17, Gorbachev addressed the Supreme Soviet. He began by announcing his eight-point program "of reforming and strengthening the structure of government power." The measures he proposed were met with loud applause from the right wing and included, for instance:

• dissolving the Presidential Council (which included such *perestroika* stalwarts as Yakovlev, Shevardnadze, and Shatalin) and replacing it with a Security Council

• enforcing law and order by creating a special presidential body to coordinate the efforts and activities of law and order forces

• preserving the Union at any cost with the clear understanding that the republics of the U.S.S.R. "cannot part company" (Gorbachev received loud applause when he said, "Let the newborn champions of sovereignty not try to frighten us with talk about what the people desire. . . . The people have yet to be asked.")

• making a special effort to provide the army, all fighting men, with a much higher level of social security

Gorbachev called for dealing "a political defeat" to those who did not share "the people's feelings"; he also demanded that the media "rethink its role."

If anyone had any doubts as to whose hands the eight-point plan played into (as I did, being as I was a convinced Gorbachev supporter who refused to see the obvious), the speech he made following the eight-point plan was about as explicit as anything he had ever said.

First, he struck out at the "destructive elements" that were "an obstacle to society's consolidation." They were, he said, engaged in a political struggle for power. He accused them of endorsing anti-constitutional acts, ignoring the law, manipulating public opinion, attempting to discredit government institutions, especially those "that consitute the very backbone" of the Union, namely "the army, the forces of law and order." These people, said he, wished to capitalize on the tense situation in the country, they had their political agenda, their motto read: "The worse things are, the better." His target was on the left.

Gorbachev then went on to say that while he accepted certain critical remarks, he certainly did not accept the view that he had lost his sense of direction. "Perhaps some of you wish to discredit the president—that would indeed be a present to those who dream of undermining the leadership of the country and of the republics. Whose agenda is this?"

Two days before this speech, Gorbachev had met with the military—generals and officers who had been elected to office as People's Deputies. He had come away from that meeting with the distinct message that the armed forces were not happy with *perestroika* and with the liberals. Colonel Victor Alksnis had come back from that meeting with the view that Gorbachev had "lost the army."

"Prior to this meeting," said Alksnis, "only the conservative-minded generals were against *perestroika,* but yesterday we saw a deaf person talking to a blind man. People talk about the threat of a military coup? Well, the army will never go against the people, but the army has been pushed to the wall by chauvinists. If the proper measures are not taken, people will arm themselves and take to the streets. That will not be a military coup. The military will be forced to defend their human rights."

That was what triggered Gorbachev's response in his speech of November 17, when he said:

"I would like to say a few words about the armed forces.

. . . In recent times they have been subjected to an atmosphere that hinders their carrying out their state duties. I believe all of us, the president included, bear the responsibility for that. I felt that view to be true as well during my meeting with the military deputies who represent all the military zones of our country. . . .

"I do not think that the armed forces—this powerful body —should stand aloof from the process of change, but nor should anyone have the permission to try to make the armed forces the dunces of the nation, as some keep trying to do. We must and we shall put an end to attempts to discredit the army, that crucially important state institution. . . ."

Having thus doffed his cap to the armed forces, Gorbachev sang a little song about the KGB:

"We must create the conditions necessary for the effective work of our security forces whose activities are of primary importance for the country. . . . The blatant campaign being conducted against them is impermissable. The security organs, like all others, are going through a period of profound change; they are searching for a part to play; they are attempting to guarantee the country's security in extremely complex conditions."

But of all the things said by the president in that speech, the key statement was this: "We have been on the defensive more than enough. It is time to advance." One month later, at the Fourth Congress of People's Deputies, Gorbachev would repeat that statement in an even more military formula: "It is time to get out of the trenches, it is time to attack."

Many people picked up on the "come out of the trenches" call, among them Russia's grand old lady of sociology, Tatiana Zaslavskaya, a scientist with a razor-sharp mind and razor-sharp tongue. Referring to Gorbachev's statement, which she called "highly informative," she asked: "Who are we being called upon to attack? We don't know.

Yet it would be interesting to know the object of Gorbachev's campaign. And who was he defending himself against in those trenches? If the defense was against the military-industrial complex, that is one thing, but it's another if it was from the media, from those who criticized him."

Almost no one reacted, though, to Gorbachev's first call for going on the offensive.

We will probably never know whether or not the man who fired that shot on Red Square, who attempted to assassinate Gorbachev on November 7, was just some kind of nut, or a maniac who was used for a specific purpose.

Similarly, we will never know—unless Gorbachev unburdens himself publicly—to what extent that event was a factor in his move toward the right. But it was a factor, one of many. Perhaps it was not the most important one but that it was a factor is, in my opinion, indisputable.

It must have been around ten in the morning when I first called Lev Sukhanov, one of Yeltsin's closest friends and advisers. He was not in his office, said the man who picked up the phone, so I asked him to convey the message that I had called and wanted to know what Yeltsin would prefer that I do: come to the White House and work with my colleagues on the broadcast of Radio Russia, or go all out for foreign TV and radio? The man said he would get back to me. One hour later he called. "Do the foreign broadcasts," he said. "There are plenty of people around to do the Russian radio. We need someone to speak for us to the outside."

And that is what I did. I can't say how many times I was interviewed or for how many stations—certainly over thirty. Nor do I remember in what order. But even if I did, I would not presume to bore the reader with a repetition of what I said and when I said it. (Whatever and whenever, it is all on the record for anyone who cares enough to look it up.) There is one interview, however, that I will not forget and that, I think, presents an interest for others. It was the *Nightline* show seen in the United States at 11:30 P.M. New York time on August 20 (5:30 A.M. on August 21 in Moscow). But I have yet to come to that.

Somehow that second day of the coup seemed to lack events of significance. Things were happening all the time, of course, but they were not in evidence. For instance, crack military units sent from the Tula region had arrived at the Ring road encircling Moscow and had stopped, refusing to move on the Russian Parliament building. And that was not the only instance of rebellion in the army on that day. Colonel-General Pavel Grachev, commander of Soviet airborne forces, had kept stalling on orders to ready his troops for storming the White House. The commander of the Soviet air force, Colonel-General Yevgenny Shaposhnikov, went much further: When informed of a possible attack on the White House by assault helicopters, he ordered fighters to intercept and shoot down these craft should that be necessary.

Other behind-the-scenes activities were taking place. At 10 A.M. Vice President Rutskoy, Prime Minister Silayev, and de facto chairman of the Russian Parliament Khazbulatov visited Anatoly Lukyanov in the Kremlin and presented him with Yeltsin's ultimatum, calling for the junta's surrender.

The one big event was the mass rally on Independence Square in front of the White House of Russia. Some two hundred thousand people participated in the rally. They were addressed by Boris Yeltsin and Yelena Bonner, by Yevgenny Yevtushenko and Stanislav Shatalin, all apostles of *perestroika.* Two hundred thousand people . . . Was that a lot or a little? Fewer than I would have liked to see. As I drove around the city that day, going from studio to studio, I could not help being struck by how many people seemed to continue to be oblivious of the coup. I began to wonder just how many actually supported it. . . .

The answer to that question is not clear. Even now, nearly half a year after the coup, we still do not really know what percentage of the population heaved a great sigh of relief and satisfaction when they heard the news on that Monday morning of August 19. Nor will we ever know—the failure of the coup pretty much precludes the possibility of anyone's answering that question honestly. But my guess would be that at least 25 percent of the population was supportive. That is one in four people, a statistic that may strike the American reader—or any foreign reader, for that matter—as surprisingly high. How could *anyone* support this new regime which was obviously hard-line, anti-Gorbachev, anti-reform, and threatening to be quite repressive? But that should really not be all that difficult to understand.

Perestroika began in 1985 and promised the nation three things: personal security, political freedom, and a better standard of living. Initially the overwhelming majority of the Soviet people backed Gorbachev and his policies. But as the years passed, the changes were slow—if there were any. Yes, political freedom did appear. Its main expression was *glasnost*—that is, the possibility to speak out, to openly criticize without fear of repression. Along with that came the possibility to travel (provided one had the means). But as for other changes . . . People became less secure, not more so. Crime suddenly shot sky high, reaching a level unheard of before in the Soviet Union. Muggings became common, along with a host of other violent crimes. People began to fear the evening streets, steel doors became the craze as citizens looked for ways to protect their homes from murderous thieves. Suddenly the republics, once seemingly so friendly, were at each others' throats. Russians living in the Baltics and in Central Asia found themselves threatened and relegated to second-class citizenship. Armenians fled from Azerbaijan, Azerbaijanis from Armenia. The proud and powerful Union began to fall apart.

And the standard of living fell, fell, and fell. Soviets accustomed to shortages, people who were not prone to complain and who had become used to having very little, were shocked at how quickly even the most basic goods and services began to disappear. The stores were empty.

But everything *was* available—provided one had money, lots of money, and especially if one had access to dollars. Former kingpins of the underworld, of the so-called shadow economy, came out into the open as cooperators, heads of joint ventures. They flaunted their wealth, underlining the inequities of a society supposedly based on the notion that all people were indeed born equal and did have certain guaranteed rights.

Gradually, a very proud nation began to see itself as a third-rate country, a country either laughed at or pitied. Smart-ass commentators vented their spleen on television, almost rubbing their hands in glee as they described the country's criminal past and tragic present. Everything people had been brought up to believe and trust—all of it was now suspect. The sacrifices, the selfless labor—all of it had been for naught. That was the message. Would you want to hear that about your country? Would anyone?

Hurt pride, loss of direction, insulted patriotism—all of those were present and, probably worst of all, the feeling that nothing seemed to be working.

When close to 90 percent of the electorate went to the polls in 1989 to cast their ballots for the candidates of their choice, it was the first time they had actually had a choice. It was also the first time they had felt no pressure about voting or not; they feared no reprisals. There was a sense of euphoria after the elections and during the time the first Congress of People's Deputies opened. But as the people's representatives bickered and posed, as debates got bogged down in endless questions of procedure, as more and more of the People's Deputies showed themselves to be vain, inept, incompetent, incapable of formulating their thoughts, as they apparently ignored the needs of those who had elected them to office, anger and apathy spread wider and wider among the population. And as this happened, more and more people began to remember the good old days, times when things were simpler, when life was easier, when you knew exactly what tomorrow would be like because it would be like today and like yesterday.

These were just some of the feelings of some of the people who had been happy to see Gorbachev move to the right and who had hoped for a return to the past. . . .

Flashback: The Dark Days of December

On December 11, 1990, at exactly 9 P.M., *Vremya*, which was then still the one and only national evening TV news program, opened with a statement by KGB chief Vladimir Kryuchkov. Here are the highlights of that statement:

Dear comrades,

We of the security organs have been receiving an increasing number of demands from the Soviet people, who wish us to state where we stand at this fateful time for our nation. They call for decisive action in support of law and order.

First, I wish to underline the necessity and inescapability of change in our society. We support this change. But as we have moved toward our goals, we have met not only with difficulties; real and serious dangers have appeared. An all-out struggle is going on in the country, a struggle over two key issues: that of property and that of power. There are forces that would like to see those issues resolved at the people's expense.

The very existence of the Soviet Union is at stake. We see the deliberate instigation of national chauvinism, of riots and violence. . . .

An anti-communist takeover is now in the making. The KGB is aware of this plot and of the hit lists the plotters have drawn up of people who, I quote, "are to be neutralized, at the proper time."

The growth of extremely radical political movements, far from being chaotic in character, has been carefully nurtured and has precise goals. Some of these movements are morally and financially supported from abroad. . . .

Destructive elements have, in fact, moved toward economic sabotage, creating even more tension at the marketplace. Here the interests of organized crime—members of the shadow economy who use shortages to make literally billions of rubles —coincide with long-term political goals [of organized crime] —including the final breakdown of our society and state and the liquidation of Soviet government. . . .

We of the security forces have made our choice. We stand resolutely for the renovation of our entire society and for the flowering of our socialist homeland. . . .

Speaking here on the president's request, I, as chairman of the KGB, feel I must make the following statement: . . .

All KGB members believe it is their duty to stop any and all foreign special services from interfering in the country's internal affairs; this also applies to foreign organizations and groups which, supported for decades by those services, have waged and continue to wage, a secret war against the Soviet Union. . . .

The KGB calls on all honest citizens to combine their efforts in the struggle against those who threaten our socialist government, our socialist system; we call upon them to say "No" to organized crime, economic sabotage, corruption, manifestations of extremism. We promise the citizenry that the KGB will move quickly and objectively when dealing with their reports relating to these matters.

*   *   *

Kryuchkov's televised statement was watched by the entire TV population—at least 200 million people. For anyone with any knowledge of the system, it brought back fearful memories.

It was, first of all, an ultimatum to the democratic movement. Second, it was a clear statement as to where the KGB stood and what forces controlled it. Third, it was an invitation to "collaborate," to report on your neighbors, on your colleagues at work, on anyone you did not like or envied; it was an invitation to a new witch-hunt, much like those of the Stalin period. But most disturbing of all, it was done "on the president's request." Some people felt that Kryuchkov had gone too far, that the president would now react. They were wrong. Over the next few days Kryuchkov's TV debut was followed by similar speeches from Defense Minister Yazov and Minister of the Interior Pugo.

Slightly over a week later, the Fourth Congress of People's Deputies opened in Moscow and it opened with a bang. The first person to take the floor, Deputy Umalatova, a member of the Soyuz group, demanded that Gorbachev resign. She called for a vote of no confidence. While the majority of the deputies refused to even consider the motion (they voted against putting her motion to a vote), the very fact that the Congress kicked off that way was an emotional shocker to many. But it was nothing compared to what happened on December 20, when Eduard Shevardnadze addressed the 2000-plus deputies in what was probably one of the most dramatic moments of *perestroika.*

He began with a very strong statement condemning rumors concerning possible Soviet military involvement in the Persian Gulf. After Afghanistan, any idea of engaging in military conflict anywhere in the world was repugnant to all Soviets. These rumors were, therefore, extremely insidious. Stating unequivocally that the Soviet Union had no plans to send troops—"even one single man in uniform"—to fight

Iraq, the minister of foreign affairs made the point that, even though the Soviet Union had enjoyed a cordial and friendly relationship with Iraq, it could not and would not support wanton aggression. However, condemning aggression and supporting the UN resolution on Iraq and Kuwait did not mean sending troops to support the allied coalition. Yet that rumor was being actively circulated.

"Let me ask the following question," said Shevardnadze. "Is all this accidental? Is the statement made by two members of Parliament about their having gotten rid of the minister of the interior, and that now the time has come to have a reckoning with the minister of foreign affairs—is that statement also accidental? It made headlines around the world and in our press. How come these bullyboys (I call them that because my age allows me to do so; they are indeed young, they wear the shoulder straps of colonels) are so courageous as to level such accusations at a member of the Cabinet? . . . I believe the time has come to think seriously about who is backing those comrades, what this is all about. . . .

"I think back to the Supreme Soviet session when comrade Lukyanov suddenly, on his own initiative, included the treaty with the German Democratic Republic in the agenda. Was that accidental? I wasn't even in the country. . . . When I returned, I was forced to furnish explanations, and the very same people who are so vocal here today were vocal then. They accused the minister of foreign affairs of making unilateral concessions, of incompetence. Not one single person, including the chairman, stood up to say this was a disgrace, that it was dishonest, that it could never happen in a civilized country. . . .

"The democratic comrades have run for cover, the reformers have dived into the bushes. I say with total responsibility for my words that a dictatorship is coming. No one knows what kind of dictatorship it will be, who will be the dictator, what kind of rules will be established."

Then came the clincher:

"I wish to make the following statement: I am resigning. Let that be, if you will, my protest against the forthcoming dictatorship."

Talk about shock!

I distinctly remember, first, my feeling of bewilderment. What in God's name was going on, I asked myself. What did this mean?

Then bewilderment gave way to anger—an anger that I still carry with me. What the devil was Shevardnadze talking about? What was this "coming dictatorship"? If he didn't know, as he said, if, as a matter of fact, "nobody knew," if the future dictator's person was anybody's guess, then how could this man, one of Gorbachev's closest associates, abandon ship? Perhaps then he did know something? Well, if that was the case, why didn't he come out and say so? Was he unhappy with the way Gorbachev had been handling things? If so, why hadn't he made that known? He had accused the democrats of running for cover, but what was he doing? He had accused the reformers of not standing up to "the bullyboys wearing the shoulder straps of colonels," but wasn't he playing right into their hands?

Even now, so many months later, after everything that has happened since then, those questions remain unanswered. Some felt Shevardnadze was disengaging from the Gorbachev group in view of developments in his native Georgia. Should Georgia become independent, they reasoned—and that was almost a foregone conclusion—Shevardnadze's loyalties would be torn. According to that school of thought, Georgia was not only Shevardnadze's first love, it was also the focus of his political future. Should he become president of an independent Georgia, his international reputation would serve to boost him and his country into prominence he could not hope to achieve in the U.S.S.R.

Another viewpoint held by many was that with the demise

of the U.S.S.R. Shevardnadze would have no role to play whatsoever. None of the sovereign republics would have a Georgian formulating their foreign policy. Two Georgians—Stalin and Beria—had left such deep wounds that even now, forty-five years after their deaths, the idea of a Georgian being in charge at the republican level was unacceptable.

Finally, there existed a third argument that saw Shevardnadze's decision as a cold and calculated act based on his desire to disassociate himself from what he considered to be a failed policy. Shevardnadze, ran the logic, did not want to be held responsible when the shit hit the fan—as it surely would.

But whatever Shevardnadze's motives may have been, one should be ruled out: His decision was not an emotional one. I remember a conversation I had with someone who grew up with Shevardnadze in Tbilisi and later worked with him in the Central Committee. This person told me the story of how he and a few other people were brainstorming with Shevardnadze. The issue concerned the situation in Abkhazia, an autonomous area of Georgia, where the indigenous population was demanding self-rule. Shevardnadze proposed a certain approach, and in response someone said, "Eduard, you are making a mistake." Shevardnadze, according to the story, gave that person a long hard look and then said, "Listen to me and remember this: I plan everything sixty-four moves ahead. *I never make mistakes.*"

When I think about Shevardnadze's resignation, I tend to qualify it precisely as something he supposedly never commits: a mistake, a serious mistake that ultimately lessened his stature. That is what I believe now, with the advantage of hindsight. But back then his resignation was one of the most frightening things any of us who supported the change could have imagined.

In November of 1991, nearly one year after his resignation, Eduard Shevardnadze accepted Gorbachev's offer to head the U.S.S.R. Ministry of Foreign Affairs. Again, I must confess I find his decision hard to understand. The ministry he returned to is such a diminished one compared to the one he left. There is hardly any U.S.S.R. to represent. Shevardnadze can no longer speak for the country. He must keep looking over his shoulder to see the signals being fired at him from the now independent republics. That is a very inconvenient way to move; what's more, there is a real danger of walking or stepping into something very painful and/or unpleasant.

Was Mr. Shevardnadze trying to help his friend President Gorbachev? That may be the case, but why then did he jump ship in December of 1990? He must have realized how badly he was hurting Gorbachev abroad. Was his move yet another mini-episode in a continuing power struggle between Gorbachev and Yeltsin, where Shevardnadze's joining of Gorbachev somehow takes something away from Yeltsin? Or is it all much more simple, the realization on Shevardnadze's part that there is no political room for him in his native Georgia and therefore he should take whatever is available? The only person who can answer those questions is Mr. Shevardnadze himself—and he has not become known as someone who answers questions readily or candidly.

I recall seriously considering the possibility of leaving the Soviet Union. I discussed it with my wife, Katherine, and with one of my closest friends from Leningrad. It was a most painful conversation, not only because the very idea of emigrating was something that hurt, but because both my wife and I knew that Peter, our son, would refuse to leave no matter what. And that meant Katherine would stay behind; she would never leave him. So what did that mean for me? I agreed to stay. Nevertheless, Katherine and I talked about making Peter understand how dangerous things might become and how to get out, should that become necessary.

Two days after Shevardnadze's sensational resignation, KGB chief Kryuchkov took the floor. If Shevardnadze's

speech had set off most people's alarm systems, Kryuchkov's made you run for the nearest fallout shelter. He elab-
orated chillingly on the points he had made two days
earlier:

• The "destructive elements" ruining the country are
those who support the breakup of "our united federative
state." Their narrow group interests hinder the development of democracy. They wish to resolve the issue of new
types of ownership "at the people's expense."

• The West is stimulating emigration from the Soviet
Union. A special effort is being made to steal the country's
scientific and high-tech brains. This is part of a plan. These
are "the facts that we cannot ignore." Outside forces are
"putting overt and covert pressure" on the Soviet Union in
the form of "doubtful concepts and ideas" that in reality
will harm the country, not help it.

• The use of force may be necessary to restore law and
order in this country.

• As the country begins to move toward a market economy, billions of rubles are being pumped out of the pockets
of honest citizens and into the pockets of thieves. Crooks
are amassing huge sums of what is still only paper money,
but when the privatization process begins, when real estate
is put up for acquisition, they will amass great wealth—
enough capital not just for them, but for several generations
of their heirs. Nobody cares anymore for the working people.

• So-called Western partners send contaminated grain,
food with high levels of radioactivity or containing dangerous chemical components: "Almost 40 percent of all the
grain we receive is substandard."

• The present crisis has been caused by the breakdown
of previous vertical and horizontal ties. There is no choice
"but to restore the old order of things in the country's eco-

nomic life—something foreseen in the president's decree. This is a temporary, but necessary, measure."

Then Kryuchkov dropped his bomb: According to KGB information, he announced, Western businesses had accumulated some 12 billion rubles in paper money deposited in Swiss banks. He knew of dangerous plans in the West to dump that money onto the Soviet market. This would lead to hyperinflation and send the economy into a tailspin.

Two days later the head of the State Bank's Hard Currency department published an official denial, saying that the amount of paper rubles in foreign banks was more like a few million, not billion. He was simply setting the record straight, having no inkling that Kryuchkov's strategy was to create anti-Western feeling. Kryuchkov hoped that this anti-Western feeling would translate itself into anti-*perestroika* feeling, since all the proponents of change were clearly pro-Western in their political views.

And what was Gorbachev doing all this time? Nothing. Or at least nothing good. He hardly reacted to Shevardnadze's resignation, although he did say he had been "surprised" by it because he had "seriously thought about offering him the vice presidency." But he had no comment about a possible dictatorship. He had nothing to say about the "bullyboys wearing the shoulder straps of colonels." Kryuchkov's "back to the past" speech elicited no comment from Gorbachev. And when he did finally speak, it was to nominate Gennadi Yanayev for vice president of the U.S.S.R. Considering that Yanayev was to become the nominal head of the junta, this appointment takes on a special importance—all the more so when one recalls how hard Gorbachev fought to get Yanayev confirmed.

But the most amazing thing of all—something most of us learned much later, something Yanayev admitted—was that Gorbachev offered him the number-two post in the country *just two hours before nominating him!* With that staggering piece of information in mind, consider what the president of the U.S.S.R. had to say about the man he had selected as his deputy as he strode to the podium. The day was December 26, 1990. The time, 4 P.M.:

"Comrade Deputies! I present for your attention my nominee to be elected vice president of the U.S.S.R. by secret ballot, Gennadi Ivanovich Yanayev." The nomination was met by some applause. Gorbachev then gave Yanayev's bio and spoke of him as a "seasoned, mature politician, a man of principles, an active supporter of and participant in *perestroika.*"

When one of the deputies suggested that Gorbachev give Parliament a choice of two or more candidates, the president said the choice was his, that it was his constitutional right, that he was in the process of forming his "team" and that it was his responsibility. Another deputy asked Gorbachev to explain how he could have first considered Shevardnadze for this job and then nominated Yanayev—they stood, said the deputy, at opposite ends of the political spectrum.

"You are in error," retorted Gorbachev, "and you are trying to make us fall into that error with you. . . . They [Shevardnadze and Yanayev] have worked together, and their views—I can personally vouch for it—are, if not identical, very close in what concerns both domestic and foreign policy."

Still, many of the deputies were not satisfied, and Gorbachev reiterated what he had said—and then added more:

"First, he is a mature politician, a person capable of participating in discussions and taking decisions of the most important, large-scale governmental nature.

"Second, he is intimately acquainted with our domestic policies and is well grounded in foreign policy.

"Third, he is a proponent of *perestroika,* he stands for renewal. . . . Finally, I value his ability to conduct a dialogue, to communicate, to listen to others. That is his strong point."

Not even Cassandra could have predicted the irony of Gorbachev's response when he was asked how he felt about the possibility of Yanayev's replacing him, should some kind of emergency make that necessary.

"Right now I see him as vice president. But I am ready to state that, should something unexpected occur tomorrow, comrade Yanayev will not fail us. He is a reliable person, someone we can count on."

But even this strong endorsement notwithstanding, Yanayev did not receive the three-quarters majority needed for confirmation.

Gorbachev refused to take no for an answer.

"Frankly speaking," he said, "this is our last chance; if the leadership does not prove capable of achieving a breakthrough, then that leadership should leave the political arena. That, by the way, is what certain forces attempted at the beginning of this Congress. They failed, but we should not give them presents in the form of a lack of organization or a lack of resolution on our part. The fact that only 583 votes were cast against comrade Yanayev . . . allows me once again to call on the Congress to endorse my choice.

"I again nominate Gennadi Ivanovich Yanayev for vice president. He is fit for that job not only on a personal level, but also politically and in the soundness of his approach to issues. Society is in a state of flux and in this most difficult period I want someone whom I fully trust to be standing by me."

But even that extraordinary appeal did not put an end to the debate. It raged on and on, and what gradually became more and more evident was less about Yanayev's views than about how he was perceived by the *perestroika* camp of the so-called inter-regional group of deputies on the one hand, and by the Soyuz group, and the conservatives in general, on the other. It was a classic case of what Soviets often call "class intuition," that is, a sense of someone's "belonging" to your team or not.

Deputy Blokhin, the leader of the Soyuz group, made that very clear:

"Comrade deputies! The Soyuz group has recently been highly critical of Mikhail Sergeyevich Gorbachev. We have mainly been concerned with the president's lack of resolution in carrying out his responsibilities. It is with that view in mind that we consider the nomination of G. I. Yanayev. In my opinion (based on my personal dealings with him), Gennadi Ivanovich is a man of principles; he stands for preserving the Soviet Union and for equality of all in our multinational country. This fully satisfies us and I call on all the Soyuz group members to support G. I. Yanayev. . . ."

Once again the issue came to a vote. The number of "Nays" had changed very little, from 583 to 563. But the number of "Ayes" had increased from 1089 to 1237—many abstainees had jumped on the Gorbachev bandwagon. Thus Gennadi Yanayev became the first vice president (and perhaps the last) in the history of the Soviet Union.

But what was the real story behind that election? Why did Gorbachev pull this rabbit out of the hat and then ferociously fight for him? The answer, curiously enough, was furnished by Gorbachev himself. On August 21, 1991, on board the plane flying him back to Moscow from the presidential resort in the Crimea where he had been held incommunicado, he participated in a discussion as to how to arrest the junta members with a minimum of risk. Such people as Kryuchkov, Yazov, and Pugo were not to be taken lightly— they could still be backed by loyal troops. "What about Yanayev?" someone asked. "Don't worry about him," said Gorbachev. "He's no problem. I'll just give him a call and tell him to give up." What that remark revealed was Gorbachev's total lack of even the slightest respect for the man he had nominated for the vice presidency, the man he had rammed down Parliament's throat. Gorbachev had picked

Yanayev because he wanted a vice president who would jump when he snapped his fingers, who would roll over and play dead when told to do so. He nominated him because he wanted a nonentity in that office.

It is very likely that Gorbachev was sick and tired of people like Yakovlev, Shevardnadze, and Bakatin, all men who had strong opinions of their own. Gorbachev was even more fed up with the likes of Stanislav Shatalin, that is, scientists and intellectuals in general, people who had not been trained in the Party ranks, as had all of his other supporters. They were experts far more knowledgeable than he was in many areas, people who refused to do his bidding and wanted an explanation as to why they should do something. He had had it with people who kept questioning everything he said or wanted to do. So he picked a typical faceless apparatchik, the kind of person he knew inside out, top to bottom.

But even there he made a mistake. It took an intellectual and a writer like Aless Adamovich, a man of passion and of conscience, to stand up in the Parliament prior to that vote, prior to Yanayev's having been nominated, prior even to the Congress's endorsement of the "special powers" that Gorbachev had been granted a month or so earlier by the Supreme Soviet, to say:

"I wish to address the following reproach to Mikhail Sergeyevich Gorbachev. We all remember how Khrushchev fell: His closest supporters, the people who supported his reforms, were alienated, gradually pushed away and out of the political arena. To lose such people as Alexander Nikolayevich Yakovlev and Eduard Ambrosiyerich Shevardnadze is tantamount to losing face, losing one's own authority and power. Should that tendency continue, there will come the day when, as we seek to find the president with our eyes, we will see instead the uniforms, the backsides, and the Astrakhan hats of generals and colonels, of military officers. . . . They will surround the president, they will take him hostage. . . . Allow me to propose the following scenario. Gorbachev was always against dictatorship, and so what will happen is, I believe, not going to be a military coup or takeover. We will grant Gorbachev the special powers he wants, then they will elect a vice president, and that vice president is the one who will take over and make use of those special powers."

Eight months later to the day, the above scenario would be played out almost exactly that way.

One of the things that became clear on the twentieth of August was that this would be the day when the army would storm the White House of Russia. How did I know that? Clearly, not because of any contacts I had with the perpetrators of the coup. The knowledge was really based on intuition. All around the White House the barricades were going up. Roads and streets were being blocked off as teams of people heaved and pushed empty buses and trolleys into strategic positions at bridge crossings and underpasses leading to that building. There was electricity in the air, a crackling kind of tension. Something was coming.

Other things were also happening, some visible, others not. For instance, the roof of the Bolshoi Theater had been turned into a series of machine gun nests by the military. This was done with a view to dispersing crowds should they assemble in the square in front of the Bolshoi or move up the street past the Metropol Hotel to attack the KGB headquarters on Dzerzhinsky Square. The military activity around the Bolshoi was clear to see. Other— much more dangerous—things were not.

At 9 A.M. of the nineteenth, Colonel Alexander Sherstyukov, a member of the Chemical Warfare Division, was summoned to the General Staff headquarters of the Soviet armed forces where he was ordered to prepare two hundred gas masks and the same number of L-1 protective anti-contamination suits. On the following day the colonel was informed of a conversation that had just taken place with General Petrov, the head of the Soviet army's Chemical Warfare troops, about the feasibility of using helicopters to spray nerve gas or any other kind of incapacitating agent on the people surrounding the Russian Parliament. The answer had been positive, and now the colonel was to keep those two hundred gas masks and suits ready for those who would need to use them.

On that same day, between two and three o'clock in the afternoon, General Achalov, deputy minister of defense for extreme situations, chaired a meeting with just one subject on the agenda: What to do about Boris Yeltsin and the government of Russia? Several points were made. First, that the Russian government had refused to comply with the Emergency Committee and that all further communication with that government was a waste of time. Second, that the Russian government had to be forced to recognize the legitimacy of the Emergency Committee. Third, that the only way to make that happen was by "changing" the leadership of the present Russian government. From that moment on, the discussion turned to purely military matters. Colonel-General Pavel Grachev, commander of the Soviet army's Airborne Forces, was ordered to assemble his men close to the United States embassy enclave behind the Russian Parliament; the Group "Alpha" (more about that yet to come), commanded by General Karpoukhin, was to move to the embankment facing the Parliament, while the Interior Forces of Boris Pugo—the dreaded OMON (an acronym for Special Missions Militia Forces)—would take up positions on Kutuzovsky Prospect. At a given hour, yet to be determined, the OMON forces would charge the crowd around the Parliament building, opening up a corridor for the Alpha group who would take the building and "do the necessary"—a euphemism for "neutralize" or "destroy." Later, in another council of war, the time for the attack was set at 2 A.M. on August 21. . . .

I got back home at about 4 P.M. My answering machine was blinking—probably more calls for interviews, I thought, as I switched it on. The first voice I heard was my son Peter's: "Hi, I'm out at the airport and I have no keys. How do I get home? If nobody's there when I get there, pick me up at Sergei's. Bye-bye."

Was I surprised! And proud! I couldn't wait to tell Katherine—and didn't have to wait very long, as she arrived a few minutes later.

"Guess what," I said. "Peter's here." She stared at me blankly, trying to understand what I had just said. Then it registered and she went white. "Oh my God, where is he?" I told her he was over at a friend's place, that I was going to pick him up and that it would be nice if she could throw together a welcome-home dinner.

That evening, as we sat and listened to Radio Russia describing what was happening around the White House, Peter told us why he had disregarded our advice: "I couldn't sit there and know that I was safe and sound, while you were threatened. I had to come back to be with you and to share with you whatever might happen, no matter what."

It is not often in life that we are deeply and unequivocally proud of our children. Some parents really never experience that feeling. Believe me, very few joys can compare to it.

We sat and listened to the voices on the radio, sometimes ebbing because of the weakness of the transmitter, and then Peter said something else that touched me:

"You remember Vilnius? You remember I was sent there to cover the story and I was put in a situation where I couldn't say anything? Where I could either lie by speaking an untruth or lie by not challenging the official line? I swore I would never allow that to happen to me again. By staying in New York and not returning now, I would have betrayed that vow. I would have lied."

Flashback: Vilnius, the Minicoup

Almost from *perestroika*'s outset, the three Baltic republics of Estonia, Latvia, and Lithuania had been a thorn in Gorbachev's side. As society opened up, as the media became more and more outspoken, the issue of the Stalin-Hitler pact, signed by Molotov and Ribbentrop in 1940, became a focal point of discussion.

Most Soviets were aware of that document's existence. After having done everything it possibly could to forge an anti-Nazi coalition with the British and the French, but having failed to do so, the Soviet leadership had no choice but to sign a nonaggression pact with Hitler. That, in short, was what was taught in school. It is a fact that France and Great Britain were reluctant to enter into any kind of agreement with Stalin; it is also a fact that the Western powers were not at all averse to seeing Hitler attack the Soviet Union. As a certain Harry S Truman was to say, "If we see that Germany is winning, we ought to help Russia, and if we see Russia is winning, we ought to help Germany, and that way let them kill as many as possible." In those circumstances it is not easy to condemn Stalin for having decided to buy time through the signing of a nonaggression pact. But what was never taught in schools, and never mentioned or categorically denied when it was brought up, was the existence of any secret protocols to that pact.

In the spring of 1987, I received a phone call from Valentin Berezhkov, a man who had been first Molotov's and then Stalin's personal interpreter from 1940 through 1944. Over the years Berezhkov had managed to stay alive precisely because he said nothing at all about what he had witnessed. Even during the first *perestroika* years he had been very guarded in his statements. So now, when I heard him say, "The time has come for me to speak," I felt a surge of excitement.

Two days later a unit headed by film director Ksenia Shergova and I were in Berezhkov's apartment for the first of three interviews, each of which would last for about six hours. The result of this work was a documentary—two one-hour specials—called *The Witness.* Although the film was ready for showing by November of 1987, it took six months to get it on the air. It also took the personal okay by Alexander Yakovlev, who at that time was responsible for the Communist Party's international relations activities. The main difficulties we faced in getting this unique piece of history on the air had to do with the part relating how the Baltic States had been incorporated into the Soviet Union as a result of the secret protocols to the Hitler-Stalin Pact.

The first person whom we had to pass the film by was Leonid Kravchenko, then deputy chairman of Gosteleradio. He did not balk at the parallel between Stalin and Hitler, but his reaction to the secret protocol part was unconditional: When they see this in the Baltics, they will revolt. I will not allow it.

When Kravchenko left TV to become the director of Tass, his place was taken by Vladimir Popov, an old-time party functionary who had worked in the Central Committee under Yuri Andropov years before Andropov became the chairman of the KGB. Subsequently Popov was appointed deputy minister of culture, a post he took great pride in, for it allowed him to play the role of Russian intellectual and connoisseur of the arts. Popov loved to play the enlightened liberal. In fact, he was a typical apparatchik who did whatever he was told and always acted out of what he considered to be his best interests.

Like all of the upper-echelon Soviet bureaucracy, Popov was extremely sensitive to danger signals—and as soon as he saw *The Witness,* he began looking for reasons not to show it. He said it was politically explosive, that the material it contained had the potential to cause major foreign policy problems. Having said that, he gave me a big smile and said, "Why don't you call Alexander Nikolayevich (Yakovlev)? After all, international relations are his department. If he says yes, then we have no problems. Here, use my *vertushka.*" Popov handed me the very special loose-leaf telephone directory that held the names of the country's power elite, those whose position gives them access to the *vertushka* system—a special phone line devised to allow these people to contact each other directly, but makes it impossible for all others to do so. I dialed the four digits of Yakovlev's number and he picked up the phone.

I had known Yakovlev from the days when he was still ambassador to Canada, where he had been exiled by Brezhnev for an article he had published attacking anti-Semitism in the U.S.S.R. and defending the role of the intelligentsia. I certainly was not close to him, but our relationship was a good one. I explained the purpose of my call. "Send me the tape," he said, "then we'll talk."

It took nearly eight weeks of pushing and reminding on my part before I was asked to come to Yakovlev's office in the Central Committee building. He was not present at the meeting, but some six or eight of his staff were. In their presence we watched the documentary and, when it was over, I was asked to think seriously about cutting everything Berezhkov had said concerning the secret protocols. The rationale for doing that was perfect: "You call your documentary *The Witness.* Well, Berezhkov was not present when those discussions between Molotov and Ribbentrop were held, was he? He did not witness them. Remove everything that he was not a witness to. . . ."

This is how sensitive the Baltic issue was. Even someone as honest and outspoken as Yakovlev backed away from it. Later, Yakovlev was appointed to head a parliamentary commission that was asked to determine the authenticity of the secret protocols. Of course, that was a year after our conversation, *perestroika* had progressed, and the Yakovlev commission was able to come in with a clear statement indicting Stalin and his government for having made a secret deal with Hitler, a deal which allowed Stalin to take over the Baltic states.

The Baltic republics were the first to capitalize on *perestroika*, the first to move toward a multiparty system, the first to create a real, active, and powerful opposition to the traditional existing structures. They were the first to speak up for their independence, and among them Lithuania was by far the most vocal.

On November 5, 1990, just two days before the country was to celebrate the seventy-third anniversary of the Bolshevik Revolution, the newly elected government of Lithuania did something of such audacity as to seem suicidal: It declared that in the republic November 7 would no longer be considered a holiday. It would not be celebrated or marked by military parades. In response to that, the Communist Party of Lithuania, the Socialist Federation of Working People, the Council of Veterans, the "Unity" organization and others appealed to the people of Vilnius to celebrate Revolution Day. The result was a demonstration and a counterdemonstration with Lithuanians screaming "Ivan, go home!" and "Occupants!," while non-Lithuanians screamed back "Fascists!" and "Separatists!" The Lithuanians tossed coins at the non-Lithuanians—"here's money for you to buy your tickets and get out"—

while the non-Lithuanians shook their fists at the Lithuanians in futile rage.

By the end of 1990 it had become absolutely clear that
the Baltics in general and Lithuania in particular had become the focus of the pro- and anti-*perestroika* forces.
Something would have to give. The question was what.

As the evening and night of January 12 moved into the
morning hours of the thirteenth, the time bomb that had
been ticking in the Baltics finally exploded: The army
moved in, occupying the Vilnius television tower and killing
thirteen people in the process. One day later, on the morning of the fourteenth, addressing a packed chamber of Parliament, Anatoly Lukyanov, chairman of the Supreme
Soviet, invited Minister of the Interior Boris Pugo to brief
all present on what had actually occurred in the Lithuanian
capital. Pugo's report made the following points:

All was well in the republic on January 12, except for
Lithuanian television and radio, which was broadcasting in-
flammatory anti-Soviet propaganda. Lithuania's National
Salvation Committee had sent one hundred delegates to the
republic's Supreme Soviet to demand an end to the anti-
Soviet broadcasts, but seventy-six of them had been beaten
up by pro-government forces. The supporters of law and
order [the health forces, as Pugo called them], marched to
the television center and attempted to stop the campaign of
lies; there they were met by guards armed with clubs and
brass knuckles.

"The National Salvation Committee," continued the minister, "appealed for help to the military commander of the
Soviet army garrison quartered in Vilnius. In turn, the commander ordered a military unit of tanks and armored cars to
intervene. The military were fired upon by members of
Sajudis, a Lithuanian nationalist organization. One officer
was killed. Another, victim of a hand grenade, lost a leg.
The military had no choice but to return fire—first, warning
shots over the crowd and then, because they were shot at,

they retaliated. Thirteen people were killed. [Eleven died of bullet wounds, two were crushed by tanks—Pugo initially did not mention that.] One hundred and sixty-three people were wounded, forty-two of whom were hospitalized, including three belonging to the forces of law and order.

"These are preliminary findings," finished the minister. "The Interior forces have been instructed to hold the radio and television center. The situation is under control."

This was the first time anyone had ever heard about the National Salvation Committee of Lithuania. What was that about? Who were its leaders? And since when could an unknown committee, regardless of who had organized it, tell the army what to do? Pressed by many deputies, Pugo was forced to admit that neither the president, nor any other representative of the Central Government in Moscow had ordered the use of military force in Vilnius. This had been, he repeated, the decision of the local commander—a decision he had taken at the request of the National Salvation Committee. No, said Minister Pugo, he did not know who the members of that Committee were. (On the following day Pugo admitted that he did know who they were, but could not give out any names—for fear of those people being attacked.) Nevertheless, he stated his belief that the army had "acted quite properly." As for the bloodshed, the blame lay squarely with the government of Lithuania, which refused to obey the Soviet constitution.

Marshal Yazov, minister of defense, accused the Lithuanian government of provoking the people and the army. He also justified what the military had done. They were, he said, placed in an impossible situation: On one side there were the pro-government Sajudis forces, all armed to the teeth, on the other, the unarmed opposition. These people had to be protected. Marshal Yazov stated that he, too, did not know anything about the members of the National Salvation Committee. However, the garrison commander had done the right thing when he decided to use his troops to protect and support the National Salvation Committee.

Yazov, head of the Soviet military establishment, was asked to explain why the television tower had been stormed and taken at 2 A.M., well after the vote by the U.S.S.R.'s Parliament to send a special delegation to Vilnius. He repeated the story about protecting the National Salvation Committee. He also stated that additional military units had been sent in the past days to the Baltics (he forgot to tell his audience these were crack paratroop forces) because of local attempts to boycott the national military service. The only way to deal with such anti-constitutional activities, said Yazov, was to use force.

On the following day, January 15, President Gorbachev addressed the deputies on the subject of Vilnius. The essence of his statement was that the roots of these unhappy events stretched back to March 1990, when the Supreme Soviet of Lithuania, in advance of the opening of the U.S.S.R. Congress of People's Deputies, passed a decree declaring the Soviet constitution null and void in the territory of Lithuania. That was nothing less, said Gorbachev, than an anti-constitutional coup.

In Gorbachev's analysis, total disregard for the constitution and the laws of the land led to the building of a critical mass of dissatisfaction. At first it was limited mainly to the Russians and Poles living in Lithuania (they made up about 15 percent of the population). But many Lithuanians also had become disillusioned with their government. To make matters worse, said Gorbachev, armed paramilitary units had been formed—they came under something called The Department for the Protection of the Country, and their existence was unconstitutional. Many of those who had signed up for duty were people who had ties to the old regime, the pre-Soviet period. They sought revenge. According to Gorbachev, lists of names had been discovered, names of people who were considered to be pro-Soviet and who were to be branded as enemies of the Lithuanian people. "Things have gone too far," said the president. . . .

This was a very different Gorbachev from the one who had started the process of *perestroika*. This was a Gorbachev who was seemingly fed up with the "so-called democrats" and who decided that the only way to get things done was to work with the hard-liners. This was also the Gorbachev who absolutely refused to have anything to do with Boris Yeltsin.

Yeltsin had called a news conference the day after the Vilnius events. There, in the presence of several hundred people, including myself, he compared what had happened in Vilnius with "the Tbilisi scenario." The comparison, he said, was valid, especially considering that both the president of the U.S.S.R. and the minister of defense had stated that they had given no orders to use military force in Vilnius. "But when I asked Yazov whether or not such an order could have been issued at the local level, he answered in the affirmative—which, as you all recall, is precisely what supposedly happened in Tbilisi."

Yeltsin refused to say whether or not he held President Gorbachev responsible for what had taken place, saying he did not have sufficient data to make that judgment. He did state, however, that in his opinion the president was under tremendous pressure from the Right. "I feel," said Yeltsin, "that the country's leadership, influenced by certain forces, has concluded it will be impossible to resolve our problems through democratic measures and that the time has come to rule with a hand of iron."

Boris Yeltsin also made another statement which, since then, has quietly been forgotten by both the Soviet and the U.S. establishments. He informed all present that he had met with U.S. Ambassador Jack Matlock immediately after the Vilnius events. "I told him that in my view the leadership of the United States lacked a full understanding of what is going on in our country. America is making a basic strategic mistake in failing to recognize the independence movement in the republics, the movement of power, political included, from the Center to the republics."

"Bloody Sunday," as that day came to be called in Lithuania, was initially presented to the people as "something that happened." No one planned it, no one was behind it. It was a tragic event, and if anyone was to blame, it was the Lithuanian leadership. But as time passed, a very different kind of picture emerged.

To begin with, Lithuania was getting out of hand. It was in the process of breaking away and, if it succeeded, its example would almost certainly be overpoweringly attractive to many of the other republics. In Lithuania, tension was mounting between the non-Lithuanians, that is, the Russian and Polish population on the one hand, and the Lithuanians on the other. Matters were made worse by increasingly empty stores and severe price hikes.

The president of Lithuania, Vytautas Landsbergis, a man of authoritarian outlook, unbending and uncompromising, added fuel to an already burning fire. There are ample reasons to believe that the local Communist Party organization, backed by the KGB in Moscow, decided that the time had come to overthrow the Landsbergis government. With that in mind, the so-called National Salvation Committee was "organized" on January 11, just twenty-four hours before the military moved in.

Among the fourteen people who were killed (that was the final count), thirteen were Lithuanians and one turned out to be an officer by the name of Victor Shatskikh. Initially, the army refused to take any responsibility for him: There was no such officer in any of the military units anywhere in the Soviet Union. Finally, thanks to good investigative work on the part of several journalists, the KGB was forced to admit that officer Shatskikh was "one of theirs." What was a KGB officer doing storming the Vilnius TV tower?

That story came out only much later. Shatskikh belonged

to an elite KGB unit called Group Alpha or the A-Team. More will be said about this secret military force in a subsequent chapter. What should be kept in mind at this time is that had it not been for the death of Shatskikh, no one would have known about KGB involvement in Vilnius.

The local Communist Party leadership, along with their Moscow supporters, probably believed that because of the price hikes and because of the frustration with some of Landsbergis's policies, the majority of the people in Vilnius would support them. They miscalculated and failed to overthrow the Lithuanian government. But they did partially succeed, for the army continued to occupy the TV tower for eight long months.

It was a minicoup. Had Gorbachev reacted to it as such, there would have probably been no coup in August 1991.

"All of you who care for Russia, all of you who stand for freedom, come to the White House of Russia. We don't want children or women, we call on able-bodied men. We also ask you to bring food, hot coffee and tea, cigarettes. It's been a long day and it will be a longer night, maybe a tragic one. We know they are planning to attack after midnight, so give us your help and your hearts. . . ." This message was repeated over Radio Russia, repeated again and again, different words, different voices, but all with the same common meaning.

At eleven I hugged Katherine and dressed. She knew where I was going but said nothing. Peter was sound asleep, victim of jet lag. We hugged and Katherine whispered, "Be careful." I nodded.

The rain was still coming down. It was a dismal night. I waved at the security guard standing in front of the Patriarch's home and walked toward the Garden Ring. There was no sense trying to drive the car—I would never get through. On the Garden Ring I turned right and started to walk, when a taxi appeared out of nowhere and braked next to me. "Need a lift?" the driver asked. I could have imagined anything but that. Moscow taxi drivers are notorious for hardly ever stopping, no matter how hard you wave at them. When they do stop, they demand to know where you are going; then they either shake their heads and drive away, or—the meter be damned—tell you their price. In recent months they had been asking for the most outrageous sums of money. The only way to guarantee a ride was to offer dollars or a pack of Marlboros. So what was this driver's angle, I wondered.

"Not really," I said. "I'm going to the White House."

"Hop in," said the driver.

And hop in I did. It was only a two-minute drive from where we were to Kalininsky Prospect, where I had to get out because of the barricades.

"How much?" I asked.

"Nothing," the driver said. "Anyone who goes to the White House tonight, we drive 'em free." He raised his fist. "To freedom."

"To freedom," I answered, and got out.

I walked down the slope from Kalininsky Prospect to the former Comecon building, past its blank dark-blue glass-and-steel facade. All along the way an endless barricade manned by what seemed like thousands of people stretched to the Borodin Bridge. People recognized me as I approached the barrier, waved, grabbed my hands and shook them, letting me through. The scene somehow reminded me of Rembrandt's *The Night Watch*. It depicts the citizens of a town preparing for the onslaught of an enemy. Boys scurry here and there, women cling to their men, while the men are no longer really there. They are, in their minds, at the town walls, ready to repulse the foe. They bare their teeth, white and flashing in the darkness, in fierce smiles. Their eyes glint, their gestures—what we would now call body language—bespeak a kind of abandon, a furious and yet joyous passion yet to be unleashed. One hears the clanging of the armor, the snorting of the horses, the barking laughter of the men and the weeping of the women.

Here, too, one could feel the tension, the readiness to stand firm, to repulse any attacker. One, too, could feel the abandon, the sense of people having cut themselves free from whatever it was that had held them prisoner before. They would never allow that to happen again. They would die before they would allow it.

The faces were young. Men in their early and mid twenties, teenagers, people in Afghan battle fatigues, some with bandannas tied around their heads, all overwhelmingly young. For years and years the media, the sociologists, and the politicians had bemoaned the apathy of the younger generation. Its members had been accused of being indifferent to the needs of their society, of being apolitical, of caring only about their personal egoistic desires.

Now, here they were. The statement was clear: They would never accept to live the way their parents had, or their grandparents before them.

I moved through the crowd, studying the faces etched here and there by the flickering flames of small bonfires. I could not help being struck by how beautiful those faces were. How noble. How pure. Transformed by the purpose of their intentions, these young people, some fifty to seventy thousand of them, were making history for a brief moment in time. They were changing their country's fate —and somehow in a mysterious way History, that greatest of all painters, was doing their collective portrait, showing us not just the face as some photo would, but bringing out the character underlying the features.

I moved through the crowd, stopping every now and then to ask people what had brought them here. I recorded many of those impromptu interviews, but saved only one. Most people just shrugged and smiled. Others had real problems trying to put their feelings into words. Not so this young man:

"Your name is? . . ."

"Yulii Novik."

"You have come here to protect Yeltsin?"

"No."

"Then why are you here? For your country?"

"No. I am here for myself."

"Could you explain that?"

"Sure. I am like everybody else in this sorry excuse for a country. I went to school, graduated, went on to university, became an engineer, got a job, did pretty well, became chief engineer when I was only twenty-seven. And I hated every minute of what I did. You know why? Because I saw that nobody gave a shit about work. Nobody was interested in anything except beating drums about fulfilling the plan. We never fulfilled it, mind you. We played around with the stats, we lied, we stuck a pillow here, padded a little there. Christ, we laughed at how we were fooling the government, and we stole from ourselves. We lived in a world that stood on its head and thought that was the only way to live.

"Then along came Gorbachev—and everything changed. I founded a co-op. I started doing work that I loved. I started respecting myself for what I was doing. I started making real money, instead of pretending to work for pretended pay. I discovered who I was. I got married and I had a son—and I want him to be proud of his father and of himself. That is what I am here for. For myself, for my son, for the right to be what I can be. I will die for that, trust me."

I had just switched off the tape recorder when a cry went up. I turned and started pushing my way toward the commotion. Gradually the sounds became intelligible words: "Dead! . . . Dead! . . . The whoresons killed them! . . . Damn their souls in hell!" Suddenly I saw my friend Mark. He was standing there crying, the tears rolling down his face and dripping off his moustache as, like a child, he rubbed his eyes with his fists, trying to stop the tears. "Marik, Marik," I called, using the diminutive. "What's wrong? What happened?"

He looked up, recognized me, hugged me, pressing his face against my shoulder, his body shaking. "God, I saw them die, I saw them die."

"Who? Who?"

"Three boys, they tried to stop the tanks, they threw tarpaulins over one of them . . . the tanks lost direction . . . one started spinning around and it crushed a boy. And then an officer jumped out and started screaming about letting them through or he'd shoot everyone in sight. Then someone threw a Molotov cocktail and one of the tanks caught fire. Oh God, then the officer started shooting. . . ."

Mark stood there sobbing. Then he suddenly stopped, looked deeply into my eyes and said, "They will never give up their power and privileges. They will kill us all."

Flashback: Here Comes the Military-Industrial Complex

Many years ago, when the Cold War was at its coldest, when the media on both sides of the political fence were far less concerned with information than with ideology, when the idea was to get through the message about who the bad guys were and who the good guys were, there was a Washington-based Tass bureau chief whose field of expertise was the American military-industrial complex. Every time he filed a report—and he filed often—the story would boil down to the military-industrial complex, the center of all evil in the United States. Things got to the point where he was nicknamed VPK (the Russian for MIC) by his colleagues.

Some years later, when he was running the North American Service of Radio Moscow where I worked, he addressed a general Party meeting (I think the subject was the role of journalists in the present political situation or some such thing). Looking out over the main conference room that seated some 350 people, he opened with the following words:

"One day, when I was the Tass bureau chief in Washington, I was walking along the banks of the Potomac River and who do you think I suddenly saw? . . ."

He paused for greater effect, and in the stillness a voice rang out: "The military-industrial complex!"—and this was followed by laughter so loud and long that the speaker became absolutely speechless with rage and stormed out of the conference room.

I am reminded of that story as I think back to the time when I would actually have argued that in the Soviet Union there was no military-industrial complex. And how would I have made that case? Well, I would have stated that in the absence of private ownership there was no room for a military-industrial complex; after all, no one could amass personal wealth through the production of military equipment.

On those grounds I would also have explained why the Soviet Union, which had a far smaller GNP than the United States, could afford to spend so much less on defense than the United States did (see the official government statistics), but still keep up with the United States militarily. Motivated by profit and super-profit incentives, I would have said, the people who own and run the military-industrial complex in the United States rip off the government and by the same token the American people who foot the defense bill: They sell the government a toilet seat for $700. That could never happen in the Soviet Union, where all prices are government controlled. That same toilet seat would probably cost 7 rubles. I don't mean to say that our military expenses are one hundred times lower than those of the United States, but you see my point.

And it is a nice point; what's more, it's true—but only up to a point. Labor was much cheaper in the Soviet Union, production costs were lower, all industries were state owned and, yes, until recently all prices were government controlled (they still are in what applies to defense-related production). But according to conservative estimates, the Soviet Union spent no less than 25 percent of its GNP on defense, while more realistic assessments put the figure at 50 percent or even higher. There was a very strong force pulling for these monstrous expenditures, and that force was one of the most powerful and most privileged in the country: the military-industrial *commission.*

Privileges had not a little to do with the opposition to Gorbachev's reforms which, as they evolved, not only opened the floodgates of criticism on the part of the press—privileges and the privileged became a prime target—but in fact threatened to undermine the whole system of privileges that had been born early on in the Soviet Union and had been perfected by Stalin.

At the risk of being redundant I would like to share with you the thought that every system develops its type of privileges. For instance, the privilege of being a free man in a slave society; the privilege of noble birth in a feudal society; the privilege of wealth in a capitalist society. In all three the privilege cannot be taken away; it is yours—even to pass on to your children. Stalin came up with something different.

In the Soviet Union, wealth had nothing to do with any kind of privilege. You could not buy your way into the system that opened up all kinds of wonderful doors. You might try to bribe someone who could open a door or two for you, but that was risky. The real way to privileges was to occupy as important a post as possible in the Party hierarchy, in the government, or in some other walk of life. The point is that *your privileges came with your position,* your job. Take your job away—and bye-bye privileges! No more summer country home, no more special resorts and spas on the Black Sea coast, no more special hospitals and clinics for you and your family, no more special stores where you could get much better food and much nicer clothing for much less money. You did not have to stand in line because the privilege system kept you in line, made you loyal. It was also a very powerful incentive for supporting the Party and for trying to get ahead in life. And it was, for sure, a source of the most terrible corruption. Differing from the privileges of the moneyed in a capitalist system, it led to greater and greater dependence of the individual on the system.

Of all the sectors of the economy the most privileged was the defense sector. From those who ran it to those who worked in the plants, all enjoyed a far better quality of life than their counterparts elsewhere. And of all the professions, the military—especially the top brass—were also among the most privileged. In fact, somewhere along the way at the apex of the pyramid, the top people—defense-related, military, Party, government—all came together. One of the most stunning examples of this was the so-called Paradise Company.

This was a group of top military people who had retired from active duty or who had "been retired," such as the former Defense Minister Sokolov and Commander in Chief of Air Defense Koldunov, both of whom had been sacked by Gorbachev after Mathias Rust, the German youth, landed his plane in Red Square. The people who were appointed to this "company" were given the title of general inspector—but not before being endorsed by the Central Committee followed by an okay from the Ministry of Defense. The members of this elite group had cars with drivers at their disposal, country homes furnished virtually for nothing, free telephone and telegraph services, a personal "hot line." Their pay amounted to no less than 80 percent of what they had received while on active duty. As general inspectors of the armed forces they had spacious offices in one of the Defense Ministry buildings, but they hardly ever went there, especially during the summer. As of the beginning of 1991, the Paradise Company (its denigrating nickname came from the army) counted 57 men, among them 22 marshals, 4 admirals, 29 four-star generals, and 2 civilians—a former Politburo member who headed the Military-Industrial Commission, and a man who ran the country's chief defense industries.

To make a long story short, being part of the military-industrial establishment in the Soviet Union meant enjoying prestige, having power and living better than most people. And just as the U.S. military-industrial complex will do just about anything to keep the money and the orders coming, to get the Congress and the government to keep on oiling the defense machinery (which is certainly a part of what the war against Iraq was about), so has the Soviet military-industrial establishment done its best to stay on top—and that, in part, was what the war in Afghanistan was about.

The "radical economic reform" championed by people like Shatalin and Yavlinsky threatened to end the status quo so enjoyed by the military and those who headed the defense industries and laboratories—and they were not about to allow that. Today we know the extent to which the KGB and the Defense Ministry worked with local Party leadership in the attempt to overthrow the legal government of Lithuania. That was in the early-morning hours of January 13. On the following day, President Gorbachev nominated Valentin Pavlov to head the new Cabinet. This nomination, said Gorbachev, had been the result of "many consultations" and "deep thought" (clearly differing from his choice of Vice President Yanayev). If that was true, then one would have to say that Gorbachev was doing everything he could to preserve the old economic structure and policies.

Pavlov, who had risen from his appointment as chairman of the State Pricing Committee in 1986 to minister of finance in 1989, had demonstrated a clear-cut preference for command economy methods. In fact, his monetary policies had been a disaster. Although Pavlov was quick to inform the Supreme Soviet session that during his tenure "no prices had been raised," he was telling much less than the truth. Pavlov had not jacked up prices, but his policies had led to price increases—they went up as the result of the price-reform program he had pushed through when he was head of the Pricing Committee. Later, Minister of Finance Pavlov's economic policies brought things to a state where the country's internal debt passed the 550-billion-ruble mark—more than two thirds of the nation's annual GNP.

There was another piece of information about which Pavlov said nothing, namely that his previous job as the man who determined national price policies, to say nothing of his post as minister of finance, automatically made him a key member of the military-industrial complex.

The idea of having Pavlov as prime minister was bad enough, but even worse were the president's four nominees to the posts of deputy prime minister: Three of them came from the military-industrial complex. All of them were part and parcel of the system. As Pavlov said when speaking at a news conference on the day after the Supreme Soviet confirmed him, "There is nothing wrong with the system. The problem is the people."

Pavlov also expressed not a little scorn for foreign aid— something that became apparent when the Swedish Radio correspondent asked him how he felt about the possibility of the flow of Western aid drying up because of what had happened in the Baltics. "As far as I am concerned," said the prime minister, "I have always regarded such aid, especially shipments of food, as a political factor, as a symbol of a change in relations. As for its economic importance, let me point out that all of Germany's alimentary aid amounts to only part of Moscow's daily consumption."

Pavlov's first move in his capacity as prime minister instantly made him the most hated man in the entire Soviet Union. Shortly after the New Year, when rumors had begun to circulate that all 50- and 100-ruble notes were going to be taken off the market and replaced with new ones, the population almost immediately made a run on the banks to change their bank notes to smaller denominations of 25 and 10. To counter that, the chairman of the State Bank went on the evening news to denounce the rumors. He also said he would be willing to "chop off his left hand . . . or even both hands" if the new-bills-for-old-bills talk was true.

Only a very few days later he should have joined the ranks of the physically disabled: An official statement, carried by the TV evening news, informed the population that people had three days to bring all their 50- and 100-ruble bank notes to their place of work and hand them in.

People went berserk. Several senior citizens died of heart attacks, believing their entire life's savings had been wiped out. Prime Minister Pavlov made a statement explaining why this decision had been necessary. First, he repeated Kryuchkov's earlier allegations: Foreign banks in collusion with certain Soviet banks had bought up billions' worth of rubles—they were preparing to dump those rubles on the internal market. This would lead to hyperinflation, which in turn would lead to the downfall of the government and of the president himself. In other words, the prime minister was the savior of both his government and his president. The second reason for reform, according to Pavlov, was to hit organized crime. The syndicates supposedly preferred 100-ruble bank notes to all others and were leery of keeping their money in banks; now they would lose that money, since they clearly were not about to try to change it officially. But Pavlov was lying on both counts—and he knew it.

It was once again the State Bank that repudiated the first count, i.e., that "billions of rubles" were sitting in Swiss banks. Its chairman pounded his table with both hands as he insisted that the maximum amount of rubles in Western banks amounted to 200 or 300 million. One should at this point ask: Why were Soviet bank managers so quick to give the lie, first to the head of the KGB and then to their boss, the prime minister? They could hardly have been motivated by their unquenchable thirst for truth. . . .

The answer, most probably, lies in the illegal purchase of foreign goods by the State Bank. Although the Soviet ruble was not (and still is not) a hard currency, that is, a currency officially accepted by any and all banks, and even though it has been called worthless, the truth of the matter is that the ruble has been exchanged for dollars and other currencies, as well as for goods. These operations, called transfers, reflect a currency's strength or weakness. According to information I have from generally reliable sources, the Communist Party of the Soviet Union secretly transferred over *200 billion* rubles at an exchange rate of 18 to the dollar; those dollars wound up in special accounts abroad. It would seem to me that the chairman of the State Bank and the head of the Hard Currency department, had to know about such transfers. So what they were doing was covering up for the Party. What they also had to know was that the bank-note reform could not affect those transferred rubles —the recipients of those rubles would certainly have been warned well in advance of the forthcoming reform by those who knew everything about it—Messrs. Grashchenko and Co.

As for striking a blow against organized crime, the very idea had the population in stitches. With the kind of corruption that had existed in the country for so many years, the underground world had influence in just about every top office in the land. The printing of new 50- and 100-ruble bank notes was an operation that had to involve several hundred people. There is no way that a few key figures had not been bribed by the crime syndicate, which could easily afford to offer a few million rubles to anyone who cared to divulge the most secret information.

The only people who were really hurt by the reform were the "little folk," pensioners and those who kept everything they had managed to put aside in savings banks, whose assets were frozen (that was part of the "reform") for about a month. Pavlov triumphantly announced that some 8 billion rubles had been taken out of circulation as a result of his brilliant measure—actually, a puny 5 percent of the money circulating in the country.

This Pavlovian reform succeeded in doing only one thing: increasing the frustration and bitterness of a population that was coming closer and closer to total disillusionment with *perestroika*. And to make sure that nobody got any bright ideas about protests or demonstrations, President Gorbachev gave his approval to a joint order, dated January 28 and signed by police chief Pugo and military head Yazov, announcing that as of February 1 city streets throughout the country would be jointly patrolled by the police and the military, both carrying assault weapons and, where and when necessary, backed up by armored vehicles. This measure, we were told, should be understood as a special effort on the part of the law-and-order forces to combat crime in the streets.

Tanks to battle crime? Very few people accepted that line. In fact, quite a few saw it as the first step toward the dictatorship that Shevardnadze had warned us about. What later came out, thanks to investigative work by journalists, was that the Pugo-Yazov order had actually been signed a full month before it was made public, that is, a week after Shevardnadze's resignation. It is quite likely that he knew of its preparation. After all, he was still a member of the all-powerful Poliburo.

If the first month of the year was any indication of what to expect, the outlook had to be bleak. . . .

It was well past 1 A.M. The tension had never abated, but no attack had yet come. I had a *Nightline* to do at 5:30 that morning and wanted to look presentable. I walked home. Along the way I met a military patrol. The officer stopped me and said, "Don't you know a curfew is in force?" I said I knew, but as a journalist had to be out and about. The officer took me aside and said, "Look, be careful. I am supposed to arrest anyone I find in the streets who does not have a special pass. I think General Kalinin is crazy. But don't tell anyone I said that. Good night." He snapped off a smart salute.

WEDNESDAY, AUGUST 21, 1991

I woke up with a start. It was 4 A.M. Katherine was not beside me in bed. Heart pounding, I got up, pulled on my bathrobe, and opened our bedroom door. Lights were on everywhere. From where I was, on the second floor of our apartment, I could hear Peter's voice coming up from the kitchen. I skipped down the stairs and hurried down the hall, where the two of them, also in bathrobes, were listening to Radio Russia. I must have looked very worried, because Katherine said, "It's okay. They never attacked."

"And they won't," said Peter. "I know their habits. They like to move under cover of darkness. Their favorite time is between two and three in the morning. Now it's light. They won't move."

Peter was right.

At about 2 A.M., two of the Soviet armed forces' crack units, the Taman and Kantemirovsky divisions, began pulling out of Moscow. Two hours later, around four in the morning, the OMON units that had surrounded the Moscow Municipality Building also pulled out. Another piece of news on Radio Russia made me smile: The Patriarch of the Russian Orthodox Church had publicly demanded that Gorbachev be allowed to address the nation on television. . . .

I couldn't help but think of that first day of the coup which coincided with the opening of the first-ever Congress of Compatriots. Several hundred people of Russian origin, some who had fled in the early postrevolutionary years, many others who had been born into Russian immigrant families in Paris and Berlin, London and New York, had assembled in Moscow; they had all gathered in one of the cathedrals of Moscow's Kremlin and had listened to a sermon by the Patriarch. Had he seen fit to raise his voice in protest? Had he called on this congregation to bear testimony to the criminal seizure of power on the part of a group of plotters? No, he had not. For him and his Church it had been, as always, business as usual.

Now, though, something had changed. Did his Holiness have access to information I was not aware of?

I wondered why the attack had never materialized. Were they bringing in additional forces? I had heard rumors about the 72nd Airborne Division's being moved to Moscow. Was that just a question of troop reenforcements, or was it something else, something much more important?

An hour later a car from the ABC bureau was there to pick me up. The driver, a young Russian, was in a good mood.

"So, Vladimir Vladimirovich, are we going to win this one?" he asked.

"What do you think?" I countered.

"You bet we will! Those *moudaks* would take second place at a world *moudak* championship." (For the edification of the reader, the Russian word *moudak*—emphasis on the second syllable, please—is a very specific term used to define a castrated ram, much as "gelding" applies to a neutered stallion. Most Russians, though, have little knowledge of the word's original meaning and have come to use it much like Americans use the word "asshole.")

"Why only second place?" I asked.

"You mean you don't know the joke?"

I shook my head.

"Well," said the driver, "that is what one lady told her husband. 'You're such a *moudak,*' she told him, 'that you would come in second at a world *moudak* championship.' So he asked her, how come only second? 'Because,' she said, 'you are such a sorrowful *moudak* that you couldn't win first place.' "

The ABC bureau is located on Kutuzovsky Prospect in one of several buildings that were built by the Soviet authorities as a kind of ghetto to keep all foreigners together and under the watchful eye of the police. It was also a way of keeping an eye on any Soviet citizens who tried to contact foreign journalists. While *perestroika* has changed much of that, the houses remain almost exclusively inhabited by foreigners, and militiamen are still posted at the entry—although more to protect the residents from muggers and their cars from theft than for any other reason.

The bureau was a madhouse. People were running in and out, many had clearly not had much sleep over the past three days. I don't remember exactly how it came up, but I learned I would be on *Nightline* with Colonel Victor Alksnis. If I had not been as tired and as wired as I was, I would probably have reacted differently. But this morning I was not completely myself. "I won't go on with him," I said. "The man is a criminal; he has no legitimate right to be on. Make your choice, it's either him or me."

I must say the ABC people handled the situation very well. They put me on the phone with their producer in New York, who proposed a compromise: We would go on together, but would have no verbal contact. They would come to me first, then let me go, then talk to Alksnis. I agreed.

I don't remember exactly what I said during the discussion, but whatever it was, it was far less interesting than what followed. Victor Alksnis had been quoted as reacting to the news about the coup by saying: "At last!" He had been gung ho and, I am sure, had celebrated this victory with his Soyuz buddies. But this morning I saw a transformation. "I am not sure the State Committee on the State of Emergency is legitimate," he said, making me shake my head in disbelief. "I can't really tell you how I stand on this, only the U.S.S.R. Supreme Soviet can make a ruling on the legitimacy of Yanayev's taking over the presidency. Of course there is one good thing about what has happened, and that is that the Union treaty was not signed. That treaty is unconstitutional. But insofar as anything else is concerned, I can't say where I stand. . . ."

I couldn't get over it. Was this Colonel Alksnis? Was this the hawk who had clamored for Gorbachev's head, who had called for establishing a state of emergency, for shutting down all democratic institutions, media, banning all parties? Something had happened. Colonel Alksnis knew something I did not know—and it was at that precise moment, at about 6 A.M. on August 21, 1991, that I first allowed myself to think that maybe, just maybe, the coup would fail.

I was not the only one to have gotten up at four in the morning: By five the entire Emergency Committee, headed by Yanayev, was in session. The coup, they realized, had failed—now they were trying to salvage whatever they could. Immediately after that session, at seven,

Defense Minister Yazov assembled his commanders. Not even attempting to control his fury, Yazov called Generals Shaposhnikov and Grachev traitors for having disobeyed his orders to storm the Russian Parliament. But this attack backfired, as the navy sided with the air force and the airborne commanders. With only the army left supporting him, Yazov had no choice but to concede and sign the papers ordering all troops to leave Moscow and return to their quarters. This became public news shortly after nine. But prior to that time I knew nothing of it— whereas Alksnis, as a military man, might have known more and much earlier.

Later many said they immediately realized the leaders of the coup would never win. Straight off they "knew" it would be a matter of a few days, one week at the most, before things went back to normal. I don't believe that. Not because I felt the situation was hopeless on the morning of August 19 (and that is exactly what I felt), but because of what the plotters had going for them. They controlled the armed forces, the KGB, the police, and the Party apparatus—in short, everything.

But in addition to that, they also had going for them the steady erosion of the people's faith in *perestroika*. . . .

Flashback: Backlash

In mid-January of 1991 the Public Opinion Studies department of the Russian Parliament polled just under one thousand Muscovites. The aim of the poll was to determine whether or not attitudes had changed between November 1990 and the present time and, if they had, what were the changes. The results were, depending where you stood politically, a major triumph or a disaster.

Some of those statistics follow:

	11/90	1/91	
1. We must keep moving toward democracy	68%	51%	(agree)
2. We must enforce order, cut back on democracy	20%	39%	(agree)
3. The most popular politicians as rated on a 5-point scale			

	11/89	4/90	5/90	8/90	11/90	1/91
SHEVARDNADZE	NA	NA	NA	NA	NA	3.81
SOBCHAK	3.84	4.06	4.21	3.88	3.88	3.65
YELTSIN	3.57	3.68	3.93	4.04	4.10	3.39
GORBACHEV	3.84	3.99	3.59	3.47	3.28	2.98
POPOV	3.60	3.67	3.86	3.71	3.31	3.15

4. Percentage of popular support for parties and associations

	8/90	11/90	1/91
Communist Party of Soviet Union	13	13	26
Communist Party of Russia	6	6	5
Democratic platform	19	12	1
Social Democrats	14	9	4
Russian Democratic Party	21	17	15
Christian Democrats	3	2	3
Pamyat	1	1	1
Liberal Democrats	Under one percent		
Monarchist Party	Under one percent		

The first thing that leaps out is the conservative swing away from *perestroika* and *glasnost.* In Moscow—one of the country's most liberal-minded cities—pro-*perestroika* support fell a full 17 percent between November of 1990 and January of 1991. Only 51 percent of all Muscovites continued to back the changes; among white-collar professionals 61 percent stood for *perestroika,* but only 41 percent of blue-collar workers shared that view. Meanwhile, the desire for less democracy and more law and order had increased by a startling 19 percent.

The second inevitable conclusion was that the ratings of democracy's leading proponents had peaked in May 1990. Since then they had slid lower and lower. The one exception was Yeltsin—his highest rating had been in November. But by January he, too, was sliding down.

The third and perhaps most troubling conclusion related to the doubling of the Communist Party's support. All of the democratic movements had lost ground.

The poll reflected the population's growing disappointment with Gorbachev and his policies. On the one hand, the old ideals and beliefs had pretty much been destroyed; most of what people had to look back on was better ignored, for it was shameful. The nation's pride was badly hurt; the sense of frustration was enormous. Had *perestroika* led to quick results, had people been able to say to themselves and to others that now the country was really moving, now they could stand tall—things would have been very different. But in the absence of such movement and in the increasingly difficult economic situation, disappointment began to be replaced by anger.

Things were moving exactly as the conservatives wanted them to move—that is, hardly. Thanks to their efforts, *perestroika* had not delivered. The one exception was the media and, more broadly, the freedom to speak, to elect and be elected, to travel. But as more and more people were saying (as they quickly took the newfound freedoms for granted), you can't eat words, you can't wear them either. With millions of bureaucrats strategically placed at all levels throughout the country, the old Party apparatus continued to function the way one of my colleagues, a journalist of the old school who knew the system inside out, most succinctly put it: A Party functionary is like a bird—he can shit all over the place, but he can't clean up the mess.

But differing from any bird, the Party was deliberately messing up *perestroika* and had absolutely no intention of cleaning up anything at all.

It must have been around ten or eleven, I was still in the ABC bureau, when we heard the roar of motors from Kutuzovsky Prospect. All of us—it looked like at least twenty people to me—dashed to the windows and the little balcony overlooking the street. The roar was deafening—and it came from only three tanks. They were racing full speed ahead, away from the Borodin Bridge, sweeping past our building, each proudly flying the tricolor flag of Russia. These were part of the armored units that had refused to obey Marshal Yazov's orders, that had remained loyal to Yeltsin. Now, obviously, they felt they had accomplished their mission and were going back to their base.

People lining the sidewalk applauded, cars honked and tooted. The sky had cleared and a shining golden sun lit up the tanks and played on the blue-white-red flags. For some inexplicable reason, the picture made me think of an Impressionist painting—dots of color and sunshine splashed here and there, the objects in the painting less important than the atmosphere.

I left the compound and went down to the White House.

Thousands of people milled around flashing smiles and V-for-Victory signs. Now that the sun was out, people had shed their trench coats, windbreakers, raincoats, hats, had cast aside umbrellas, and were soaking up the late-August warmth. The barricades were still there—logs, old bathtubs, steel rods, rolls of barbed wire, chunks of reenforced concrete, piles of bricks. They would stand untouched for several days. I would revisit them several times, each time thinking to myself how romantic they looked and how futile they would have been against an organized military onslaught. Especially one spearheaded by Group Alpha, often called simply the A-Team (not to be confused with the never-ending U.S. TV series).

The A-Team was created in 1974, when Yuri Andropov headed the KGB. Its purpose was anti-terrorist activities. Initially a mere thirty men were selected for this super-elite corps. All of them had university degrees, all of them were incredible specimens of physical perfection. Their training was as intensive as it was diversified. Any of them could fly a jet fighter-bomber, command a nuclear submarine, drive a tank. But what they did best of all was kill. Rapidly, effectively, quietly. Those thirty men were the equal of a military force several hundred strong—and then some.

Initially they answered to only one man—Yuri Andropov, that is, the chairman of the KGB. Things changed, however, and soon the A-Team was put at the disposal of more and more people. It was used for different purposes that were anything but anti-terrorist in nature. It was the A-Team that took the presidential palace in Kabul. It was also the A-Team that was flown into Vilnius under the cover of darkness in unmarked planes and that stormed the Lithuanian capital's television tower and broadcasting facilities, after which the men were spirited out in the same unmarked planes. By then the team numbered up to five hundred men—all officers under the command of General Victor Karpoukhin.

The junta chose the A-Team to act as its iron fist. On August 18, the day preceding the coup (and the day when Gorbachev was visited by a "delegation" of the coupsters who demanded his support and resignation), the A-Team was urgently summoned to Moscow—supposedly to fly a mission to Armenia where a group of soldiers was being held hostage by local terrorists. Once in Moscow, the team was put on alert and kept that way until the afternoon of August 20, when General Karpoukhin informed his deputy commanders that the A-Team had been ordered to take the building of the Russian Parliament at 3 A.M. the next day. Several officers were sent out to reconnoiter the area. They came back with the following report:

1. The A-Team could accomplish its mission in a minimum of fifteen and a maximum of thirty minutes.
2. The barricades were no problem at all.
3. If any of the pro-Yeltsin tanks or armored vehicles started firing on them, the A-Team would suffer heavy casualties, but not enough to stop them from accomplishing their mission.
4. The assault called for the use of special weapons made specifically and only for the A-Team.
5. Several thousand people surrounding the Parliament would be killed.

According to subsequent interviews and reports, the A-Team's decision to disobey orders and not storm the Parliament building was based on that last factor. A-Team commander Karpoukhin tried to make people believe that it was he who called off the operation. But General Golovatov, who took over the A-Team after the coup, said that Karpoukhin had accepted the orders, had tried to bully the A-Team into going ahead with operations, but when all the officers informed him of their decision not to obey orders he had been forced to back off.

In fact, the reason why the attack never happened was the most obvious of all: These men did not want to take responsibility for spilling the blood of their brothers and sisters. As one of them told me, "My son could have been with the defenders; so could have my brother, or lover, or wife. I was not going to risk killing them." It was as simple as that. For these men politics had very little to do with their decision. Without the A-Team, without its most potent weapon, with the army divided as to where its loyalty lay, the leaders of the coup could not really hope to succeed. They gave it a try and then, when the attempt failed, they all started to back away—in a manner very similar to what had occurred in a less dramatic way in the U.S.S.R. Parliament only two months prior to these events.

Flashback: A Pavlovian Reflex

Between the end of April and mid-June of 1991, I was in the United States to co-host a month-long series of daily radio talk shows with my friend Phil Donahue. It was extremely difficult to follow the Soviet scene. To my distress, I discovered it was virtually impossible to get a fresh copy of any Soviet daily. Whereas in Moscow you had a choice of *The International Herald Tribune, USA Today, Time,* and *Newsweek,* not to mention several British, French, and German periodicals (provided you had hard currency, for they were not selling for rubles), in New York the best you could hope for was a week-old copy of *Pravda* or *Izvestia*—and even finding something like that was a real challenge. News featured on network television was (and remains) skimpy and superficial. While there was much more coverage in the press, and while that coverage had, generally speaking, gotten better, it was still far from what I needed to keep abreast of the goings-on at home.

As I look back on those months, what stands out in my memory is, first, that the Nine Plus One process picked up speed and came to be called the Novo-Ogaryovo process, thus named after the village of Novo-Ogaryovo, situated some twenty miles from Moscow, where the ten presidents and/or their representatives were meeting regularly to map out the new Union treaty. Second, when Gorbachev had gone to London to attend the Group of Seven meeting, several Lithuanian customs posts had been set on fire, thereby repeating what had definitely become a pattern since the days when the opposition headed by Ligachev took advantage of Gorbachev's trip to Yugoslavia in March of 1987 to publish Nina Andreyeva's infamous "manifesto." Third and most important, that the Russian presidential elections, set for June 12, would feature a field of runners that included, besides Yeltsin, former Prime Minister Ryzhkov, former Minister of the Interior Bakatin, and one of the country's most hard-line military figures, General Makashov. The list included a few other names which I paid absolutely no attention to—a serious mistake, as I was to discover.

As the elections drew nearer and nearer, American Kremlinologists and the leading dailies and weeklies of the United States all seemed to share the view that Yeltsin would not win on the first ballot, that is, would not receive over 50 percent of the popular vote; this would force the elections into a second-round contest between the two candidates who had picked up the largest number of votes. Predictions had Yeltsin and Ryzhkov coming in one–two after the first round; but in the second, they stipulated, the Bakatin and Makashov vote would go to Ryzhkov.

I could not believe what I was reading and hearing. One really had to be out of touch with reality, or so it seemed to me, to think Yeltsin could lose, that he would be forced into a second round of voting. I was not simply puzzled by this lack of understanding on the part of so many of my American colleagues, but also worried: If that was how they read the situation, how could they presume to furnish their readership with any kind of understanding for what was happening in the Soviet Union?

But if that absence of insight on the part of the U.S. media startled me, I was stunned when I learned that the

Communist Party leadership in the Soviet Union felt exactly the same way: They had no doubts whatsoever that Yeltsin would not win on the first ballot! I wonder whether it was not their unequivocal view that influenced American reporters who spoke to these people, as they attempted to weigh the situation.

The right wing also felt certain that Gavriil Popov and Anatoly Sobchak, two outspoken liberals who were running, respectively, for mayor of Moscow and mayor of Leningrad, would also be forced into a second round of voting, where they might lose. But that view was not altogether unjustified.

Soon after Popov and Sobchak were elected to office in 1989, both Moscow and Leningrad began to suffer badly from a lack of food. Dairy products, meat, vegetables, even bread were not reaching the stores. The explanation for this —or at least the one usually trotted out when journalists made inquiries—was that the old mechanism had been destroyed, while no new one had been set up to replace it. That sounded plausible enough, but it was not the truth or, at least, certainly not the whole truth.

What was really going on was economic warfare. The Moscow and the Leningrad *oblast* (administrative areas) were under control of their respective Party secretaries who, in turn, controlled the many regional secretaries of each *oblast.* The regional secretaries lorded it over the district secretaries. At the very top of this pyramid stood a given secretary of the Central Committee—and in the case of agricultural policy that man was Yegor Ligachev (as I mentioned earlier, Gorbachev had "demoted" him to that post). I have very good reason to believe that the food shortages in Moscow and Leningrad (as well as in Volgograd and Sverdlovsk, where democrats swept the old guard out of office) had very little to do with the breakdown of the old system or the absence of a new one. They had to do with a calculated effort on the Party's part to starve out the democrats, to artificially make the food situation even worse than it was by slowing down deliveries, decreasing production, and creating other such nuisances.

When Gorbachev had appointed Ligachev to head agriculture for the Party, I had snickered with anticipation at how Ligachev would fall flat on his face. The truth of the matter was that Ligachev and the conservative party leadership made use of the appointment to discredit the newly elected democrats. The goal was clear: Create enough dissatisfaction and anger to make the "inept liberals" lose the next elections to someone who promised to clean up the act and make things start to move.

I must say, I had my doubts as to how Popov and Sobchak would fare in the elections. Yeltsin would breeze right through, of that I was sure. But that these men could be held responsible for the additional hardships the people of Moscow and Leningrad had to deal with—that was a very different story.

I was proven to be a doubting Thomas. Much to their credit, the people gave Popov and Sobchak an overwhelming vote of confidence (well over 60 percent of the total vote). Yeltsin won in the first round, too, but with a lower popular vote: 53 percent. True, that was more than double what the number-two man, Nikolai Ryzhkov, got. With some minor qualifications, the elections were somewhat anticlimactic—except for one major surprise: the strong showing of a dark-horse candidate by the name of Vladimir Zhirinovsky. A virtual unknown, he garnered 7 percent of the popular vote (some 6,000,000 votes) and came in well ahead of such visible figures as Vadim Bakatin and General Makashov. This was not only surprising, it was also very troubling, for Vladimir Zhirinovksy was and remains a dyed-in-the-wool Russian fascist—a person and a subject I will discuss in greater detail.

* * *

Yeltsin's victory made him *the only democratically elected president in the Soviet Union.* All the other presidents, starting with Gorbachev, had been elected by their parliaments. Yeltsin had been elected by the people—and this gave him true legitimacy. Nothing could have frightened the conservatives more.

Exactly five days after the elections, on June 17, Prime Minister Valentin Pavlov was, as certain Communist Party newspapers put it, "called upon by the deputies" of the U.S.S.R. Supreme Soviet to address the subject of the critical state of the national economy and the deepening crisis in society. (Gorbachev was thrashing out the details of the Union treaty in Novo-Ogaryovo and was absent.)

Pavlov opened with the usual "we all support *perestroika*" line, after which he got down to business. In this critical situation, said the prime minister, the government must be granted the right to deal with the most pressing issues *without the president's consent,* or for that matter the consent of the Supreme Soviet.

Prime Minister Pavlov demanded that the Supreme Soviet invest him with emergency powers; also, that the government be given legislative authority in addition to executive functions.

Pavlov's speech was followed by several hours of debate and discussion, including a very revealing question-and-answer period—so revealing, in fact, that at least a few parts of it should be brought to the reader's attention:

Q. Why do you need those additional powers?

A. The president works fourteen hours a day. He bears responsibility for the many issues which he handles personally. But if he is forced to handle everything, then even forty-eight hours a day would not permit him to carry out his duties. In my opinion, the president in general should not assume too many responsibilities.

Q. We know that Gregory Yavlinsky's program* was endorsed by a group of Harvard economists. . . . How do you feel about that?

A. I know some of those Harvard gentlemen; I have met them. They do not know our conditions; they ignore our outlook on life. They have their own criteria and values, their understanding, their concepts about living and working. It does not make sense to expect them to help us understand anything at all. They would never understand why I cannot leave any potatoes or gravy on my plate. But I cannot do otherwise. Therefore it is impossible for us to have a common program.

For the first time in the history of the Soviet Union, the head of the government was not only publicly expressing disagreement with certain aspects of the head of state's policies but was asking the Parliament to help him usurp the president's authority. Many delegates were more than happy to do so. One of them expressed disbelief that the West would ever seriously aid the Soviet Union, accused the Russian Parliament of organizing artificial inflation in the country, and called on the assembly to meet the prime minister's request. Unexpectedly—at least for a great many people—the chairman of the Supreme Soviet, Anatoly Lukyanov, supposedly Gorbachev's friend of over forty years, not only supported the deputy but suggested that his speech be featured in full on national television.

But the man who put the icing on this particular anti-*perestroika* cake was none other than Colonel Alksnis. He announced that there was a conflict of interest between the president and the Supreme Soviet, and between the president and the Cabinet. In that situation, said Alksnis, we

* Yavlinsky spent several weeks working with a group of Harvard economic experts with the goal of coming up with a model suitable for the Soviet Union. That model was then presented to President Gorbachev, President Yeltsin, and other republic presidents.

Supreme Soviet deputies must side with the Cabinet, for it is working to preserve the Union of Soviet Socialist Republics.

The evening session of that same day (June 17) was no less astonishing than the morning one. In the absence of the prime minister and Chairman Lukyanov, both of whom had left that afternoon to participate in the Union treaty discussions in Novo-Ogaryovo, the deputies voted to recess the debate on Pavlov's motion until the next day. However, to "better prepare" for those debates, they called on Defense Minister Yazov, KGB chairman Kryuchkov, and Interior Minister Pugo to brief them on the state of the nation. Lo and behold, those three gentlemen, almost magically, turned out not only to be there, but even had their briefing papers ready. . . .

The briefing went on behind closed doors, but journalists were quick to go to their sources and then to compare notes. Our sources confirmed the following:

Yazov called for restoring the Soviet Union's superpower status and made it clear that he could not vouch for the armed forces if things continued to deteriorate.

Pugo quoted hair-raising figures illustrating the spiraling crime rate and suggested that honest citizens would soon be afraid to leave their homes.

Kryuchkov made it known that the CIA had finally succeeded in bringing to fruition the plot that KGB chief Yuri Andropov had uncovered in 1977. Put in simple terms, the plot went as follows: The West offers to educate the Soviet people and in so doing turns them into "Trojan horses." By 1991, said Kryuchkov, the number of Trojan horses in the country had become so great and their influence had so grown, that nothing less than a state of emergency could now save the day.

On the morning of the eighteenth, the session drafted a resolution granting Pavlov special powers. Again, as sources have it, the next step in the game was to have Gorbachev invite Pavlov to Novo-Ogaryovo to negotiate a mutually acceptable settlement. But that did not happen. Instead, Lukyanov was called into Gorbachev's office during the lunch break . . . and emerged a somewhat changed man. At the afternoon session of the Supreme Soviet, again conducted behind closed doors, Lukyanov informed the deputies that Gorbachev was "busy nailing down the last loose ends of the Union treaty" and "has asked that Pavlov's motion not be put to a vote until the president's return." That meant Gorbachev was solidly back in charge. The reaction to that was almost comical. As one source told me, "the three big bears [Yazov, Kryuchkov, Pugo] immediately developed a bad case of cold feet and announced to one and all that, far from threatening Gorbachev in their previous speeches, they had simply been expressing their concern with the state of affairs, nothing more."

Three days later, on June 21, the president appeared in Parliament and for the first time ever took the Soyuz group to task. He made it clear he was no longer on their side; he also made it clear that Pavlov did not have much of a future to look forward to—even though Pavlov was quick to announce he had never asked for anything at all, much less for special powers.

Gorbachev had finally made his choice—but a forced choice, to be sure. On the one hand, he had the future signatories of the Union treaty, a visit to London, and the news that on June 19 the United States Congress had passed a bill making aid to the U.S.S.R. contingent on human rights conduct, demilitarizing the economy, and moving toward a market economy. On the other hand, he had the interests of the Soyuz group and the conservatives to consider. The choice was preordained. Gorbachev once again veered to the left, while Lukyanov dropped his Soyuz buddies—at least temporarily.

By three in the afternoon it looked as if everything was over. The end had come with such swiftness, the forces of evil had fallen so quickly that it was almost too good to believe. I received a call from my friends in the Union of Soviet Journalists who told me there would be a mass rally at five o'clock on Dzerzhinsky Square in front of the KGB headquarters. I promised to be there.

I had never been caught in the crush of a crowd before, except once, in Tbilisi after a soccer game, when some fifty or sixty thousand people simultaneously rose from their seats and made for the exits. I will never forget the sense of helplessness as I was swept along; I had prayed for only one thing, that I would not lose my footing and be crushed by the crowd. Here, as I pushed ahead up Teatralniy Proyezd, the Metropol Hotel on my left, and the Maly Theater on my right, I discovered a different crowd. Several thousand strong, it was not the multiheaded monster I had known before; it was composed of people, individuals, men and women who smiled, nodded, waved, who allowed you to walk, who gave each other breathing space.

I looked up and suddenly saw the balcony window of the room my father, mother, younger brother, and I had occupied in the Metropol, when we had first arrived in the Soviet Union in December of 1952. We had lived there for nearly two years. . . .

Was that thirty-nine years ago? To me it seemed more like thirty-nine centuries. What would my father have thought of all this? My father the true believer, the man who gave up a great career in the United States movie industry to go back to the Soviet Union, taking his wife and two kids with him. Would he have been able to deal with the collapse of the system he so supported? Would he have felt terribly guilty for having radically changed the lives of his wife and children, making them tear up their roots, suffer the pains of rejection by a foreign culture—and all for what? I could almost see him standing there at that window, looking down at me. Was he smiling? Or was he white and grim?

The crowd stood in a semicircle around the statue of Felix Dzerzhinsky, the creator of the V.CH.K., which later became the NKVD, the MVD, the MGB and, finally, the KGB. The speakers, I among them, stood on the marble base surrounding Dzerzhinsky's pedestal, facing the crowd. There must have been at least fifteen thousand people. Why they had come here, what had drawn them are questions I will never have the answers to. There had been no announcement on the radio; the decision to have this meeting had been a spontaneous one. "Start speaking and people will come"—that had been the view expressed by someone at the Union of Journalists. But the crowd had gathered well before we got there, as if they sensed this would happen, and now thirty thousand eyes were looking on in anticipation. Eduard Sagalayev, first secretary of the union, spoke. When he announced that Marshal Yazov had committed suicide (information that had been erroneously circulated by one of the wire services), the crowd roared its approval. The thirst for revenge and blood was more than tangible.

Sagalayev was followed by one of *perestroika*'s true heroes, Alexander Yakovlev, a man who had become close to Gorbachev when the future leader was Party secretary for agriculture back in 1982. Yakovlev had stood by Gorbachev through thick and through thin; though he had been dropped by Gorbachev, his loyalty had never wavered. He had steadfastly supported the man who had started the process that had altered the face of Europe and of the world.

I must admit, I was not listening to what the speakers

said. I was looking over the crowd, transfixed by the sun as it slowly set in the west, flooding the broad avenue that led to this monument. It had become warm, the air was balmy, it had a springlike quality to it, and I found myself completely at peace with myself and my surroundings.

Then I felt someone jab me in the ribs. The crowd was chanting "Poz-ner! Poz-ner! Poz-ner!" It was—and remains—the scariest moment in my life. I took a deep breath and said:

"This may sound strange, even obscene, but bear with me. I want to thank the junta for what it did for us. . . ."

There was some laughter in the crowd, uncertain laughter.

"First, I want to thank the junta for uniting us, for finally bringing us together. Let's admit that we democrats have cared more about proving our point, each separately pulling his way, than about pulling together for democracy. Our enemies took advantage of that. Hopefully, we have learned that lesson and now we stand united.

"Second, I want to thank the junta for helping us recover our pride. Over the past three or four years our heads have hung low. The Emergency Committee played to that in its 'Appeal to the People'—remember when they brought up the shame we now feel when we go abroad? Sadly enough, they were right. What was there for us to be proud of? But now, after having saved the White House of Russia, after having looked deep into the abyss and stepped back, after having won this battle—we have the right to say: "We, too, are proud human beings, we have proven our love for democracy and freedom, we can walk tall.

"There is nothing finer than to have that feeling. It gives us the power to do whatever may be necessary to save our country. The bottom line is, we now again believe in ourselves—and that is the greatest belief of all. The sight of thousands of people standing ready to fight off tanks with their bare hands, willing to die rather than live like slaves again—that is a sight few are lucky enough to see; to witness it is to realize that nothing on this planet of ours can match the strength of free people.

"Third, I want to thank the junta for giving us back our army. If anyone had any doubts—and we know such doubts existed—about the army's attitude toward *perestroika,* about its loyalty—now we know: The armed forces are there to protect us and to help us. The army refused to obey the junta, refused to storm the White House of Russia, and thereby proved it is truly the people's army.

"And finally, let us not in our victory emulate our foes. Let them be put on trial, let them enjoy a competent defense, let their crimes be proven, let the law guide us, not retribution. Revenge leads nowhere but to more bloodshed. Enough. It is time to be human."

There was a tremendous roar. I was picked up and carried down into the crowd, where people shook my hand, slapped me on the back, hugged me. Out of the corner of my eye I saw all the others I had been up there with were getting the same treatment. Gradually the whole crowd moved down toward Manezh Square and the Moskva Hotel, where another rally was planned.

Again I thought about the new era we were entering. All the rules had changed, as had most of the players; those who had not would be playing different roles. And it was then that I suddenly wondered what would happen now between Gorbachev and Yeltsin. . . .

Flashback: "Boris, You Are Wrong!"

De jure Mikhail Gorbachev was elected general secretary at a plenary session of the Central Committee in March 1985. De facto he was elected by the members of the Politburo just a few days before the plenum.

According to Party rules, the Politburo could only recommend its candidate for the supreme post of general secretary. According to Party practice, nobody dared vote against the Politburo's decision.

When Konstantin Chernenko passed away, Gorbachev moved quickly to convene a Politburo meeting. His haste related to the absence of Vladimir Sherbitsky, first secretary of the Ukraine's Communist Party, and Dinmukhamed Kunayev, first secretary of Kazakhstan's Communist Party. Both of these powerful men were supporters of Moscow Party boss Victor Grishin. Both did their best to return to Moscow from abroad as soon as they learned of Chernenko's death. But Gorbachev acted too quickly for them. And so it came about that only nine members of the Politburo voted, instead of eleven, and the vote was five to four in Gorbachev's favor. What those figures indicate, in addition to the mind-boggling fact that what was then one of the world's most powerful leaders could be appointed in such a fashion, is that Gorbachev elected himself; he cast the decisive vote that put him in power.

One might question the veracity of what I write, for I certainly was not sitting in on the Politburo meeting when the event I have been describing occurred. Nor was any of this made public. But in a convoluted sort of way, I know what I know because of the secrecy of the proceedings, that is, because of the way information was once gathered in the Soviet Union.

Secrecy was always a prevailing feature of Soviet existence. It was the offspring of the carefully nurtured siege mentality, devised to keep people's minds busy with the foe from without and within. The enemy was everywhere, looking through keyholes, spying on you, eavesdropping on your conversations. Comrade, do not let your guard down! All information was classified: Only the chosen few had access to foreign periodicals; even fewer had access to back issues of Soviet periodicals—real knowledge of the past provided much too dangerous a possibility for a more accurate understanding of the present.

I believe it was Hegel who postulated the concept of opposites being locked in constant dialectical struggle, of opposites being inseparable parts of the one. In Soviet society, this meant that the more secretive our world became, the more it spread and fed on rumors. Official sources of information, such as the press and television, were, if not disregarded, certainly less trusted than rumors—and with good reason. Whenever a Soviet official went on television to publicly deny a rumor, experience proved him to have been lying. Along with rumor-spreading, secrecy bred inquisitiveness; it taught people to read between the lines, to interpret statements, to look for signs and symbols.

There were only nine men and a couple of secretaries present at that Politburo meeting on the fateful day when Gorbachev was elected, but I know for a fact that he won by one vote and that his contender was Victor Vasilyevich Grishin.

Not many people in the Soviet Union remember Grishin today. And yet he was a powerful figure, being not only a member of the Politburo, but also the head of Moscow's Party organization, one of the country's most coveted posts. In a centralized system such as that of the U.S.S.R., the capital, Moscow, was the alpha and omega of everything, the hub. In many ways, control of Moscow meant control of the country. *All decisions* were made in Moscow; without Moscow's imprimatur virtually nothing could be done, whether it concerned getting permission to procure spare parts for your factory or securing an exit visa to travel abroad. The head of the Moscow Party organization had always been a prominent player in the power structure and Grishin was certainly no exception.

Grishin was a typical party functionary. Too young to have participated in the Party's creation, in its struggle against tsarism, in the revolution, or in the civil war, he was one of those who had grown up and matured with the understanding that the Party's supreme power was a fact not to be questioned, a state of affairs as predictable as the flow of the seasons. More cunning than intelligent, Grishin had been shaped by the Party machine created by Stalin, a man who disliked and feared competition and who devised a system which sifted through the millions who sought to work for the Party. The system weeded out and discarded those who did not fit the necessary parameters and fed the selected many into a kind of gigantic pinball machine. Some were almost immediately knocked out of the game, others progressed a bit then were stopped, and the select few became high scorers. Of these, the elite achieved the status of Politburo members. They were the ones who had mastered the rules of the game, and of all the rules perhaps the most important was to give the impression of being a nonentity.

In a curiously sinister way, the higher these Party functionaries rose, the more they looked alike, both physically and in dress. When you saw them standing atop the Lenin Mausoleum on May Day or November 7, when the distance blurred the difference in their facial features, you found yourself studying a group of look-alikes: all short, all stocky, all wearing the same gray coats and fedoras. They were similar in many other ways: They all came from humble origins, none of them had a university degree, they all had a healthy dislike for intellectuals, their Russian was as drab as their clothing—a mixture of bureaucratese and folk lingo. Many of them had serious problems with long words or names. Nikita Khrushchev never managed to pronounce correctly Jawaharlal Nehru; Brezhnev was the subject of endless jokes for his inability to pronounce such words as "sotsialistichesky" (socialist) and "sistematichesky" (systematically). From his lips, the latter came out as "sissimassissi," an ambiguous kind of abracadabra; in English it could be rendered as "titsymatitsy." Even Gorbachev to this day cannot correctly pronounce the word "Azerbaijan" (his rendition is "Azebardjan").

But it would have been a bad, if not fatal, mistake to assume all of those Party bigwigs were as faceless and as similar as they seemed. They were not. I would even risk stating that they shared only one feature—an overwhelming desire to get to the top, combined with total unscrupulousness in how to get there.

American conservatives love to take credit for the "fall of Communism." It was all thanks to Ronald Reagan, they will tell you, to his policy of getting tough with the Russkies, of launching SDI, more commonly known as "star wars"—that was what ended the Communist empire! What self-serving stupidity; what a misleading, self-indulging understanding of history. Just one vote, one single change from a hand up to a hand held down, would have changed the world.

Ronald Reagan and the entire American right wing had nothing to do with Grishin's loss to Gorbachev. The men who then made up the Politburo—people like Gromyko and Ustinov—had built their entire careers on not giving a hoot in hell about what the rest of the world thought. They were all hard-liners in the worst sense of the word. I think that had Grishin been elected, the United States and the Soviet Union would have been at war within two or three years, maximum. Ronald Reagan's ticket to the White House had, among other things, been won on his promise to get tough with the Russians. There are not a few people who attribute the demise of communism (that is how they refer to the events of *perestroika)* to President Reagan's military buildup, to his forcing of the Soviets into an arms race they could not match. What that argument ignores are at least two things. First, that Mr. Reagan had nothing to do with Mr. Gorbachev's becoming general secretary—that should now be clear to the reader. Second, that by the time Gorbachev was elected general secretary, Ronald Reagan had been in office for slightly more than one full term. During that period he had more than fulfilled his "get tough" promise. The net result was that the relationship between the U.S.S.R. and the United States stood at an all-time low. The danger of military conflict had increased; Soviet defense production was up. Neither Brezhnev, Andropov, nor Chernenko had demonstrated the slightest inclination to back down. Victor Grishin and his supporters were of the same ilk. There is no reason at all to believe they would have been more reasonable. Conversely, there is every reason to think they would have pushed the nuclear button had they been backed into a corner.

We should all thank our lucky stars for Gorbachev's one-vote win. Thank fate, thank whatever deity or superstition we believe in. But the one group we should not thank is the American conservative establishment, which had the stupidity and arrogance to think it could play chicken with its Soviet conservative counterparts and win.

When Grishin lost to Gorbachev, he lost everything. To anyone versed in politics, especially Soviet politics, it was clear that Grishin was on his way out, along with the three other men who voted for him. Similarly, the four who backed Gorbachev could count on his support (one of the main reasons why Yegor Ligachev, one of Gorbachev's main critics and political opponents, remained in the number-two position for so long). Grishin's ouster meant Moscow would have a new Party boss handpicked by none other than the general secretary—Mikhail Gorbachev. That person turned out to be Boris Nikolayevich Yeltsin.

His appointment, as I recall it, did not create much of a

stir, except for the usual flurry of activity on the Moscow political grapevine aimed at determining what connections Yeltsin had and at what level to bring about Gorbachev's decision. As far as most people were concerned, Yeltsin was just another of those party bosses who had started out at the very bottom (in his case, as a construction worker), had displayed a combination of willpower and leadership, had been offered a Party position, and had made the best of it.

Yeltsin had become the Party leader of the Sverdlovsk *oblast* Party Committee—an extremely important position, considering that Sverdlovsk was not just one of the country's main industrial sites, but also one of its main defense industry bases. The man responsible for that city's industrial performance was more than just another *oblast* Party boss— in itself a key post, for the *oblast* secretaries were often the system's kingmakers and king-breakers. The Sverdlovsk Party boss was one of the three or four most important in the country, and Yeltsin's appointment was an indication of how well he had performed. His appointment was also an indication of the forthcoming changes in Moscow, a city that had gone from indifferent to bad under the reign of Grishin, a man who saw Moscow out of the window of his ZiL 117 limousine and cared little, if at all, for the city's condition.

Yeltsin's tenure as Moscow Party secretary earned him almost nothing but universal dislike. He was, people said, mean, uncouth, boorish, and belligerent. He swore at subordinates, banged his fist on the table, insulted colleagues, drove women to tears and, as rumor had it, one or two people to suicide. He was relentless in pursuing whoever displeased him and did not tolerate any argument.

Yeltsin was also a grandstander. Whenever he "fixed" something for the city, he did it in the most public way possible. He made a point of going to the people, making sure they saw him, shaking as many hands as possible. In a way, he was very different from the aloof and distant

Grishin; but he was also very similar in his arrogance. That, at least, was the conventional wisdom.

Then, in October of 1987, everything changed. The news reached me when I was enjoying a sauna in the resort town of Pitsunda on Georgia's Black Sea coast: Boris Yeltsin had supposedly taken the floor at a plenary session of the Central Committee and had severely criticized Mikhail Gorbachev for moving too slowly, for not pushing economic reform and, of all things, for putting his wife Raisa too much in the limelight. My initial reaction was disbelief. No Central Committee member in his right mind would openly criticize the general secretary. But Yeltsin was not simply a member of that elite body. He was secretary of the Moscow Party Committee. He was also a candidate-member of the Politburo—and as such he was someone who down the line had a good shot at becoming general secretary. He had to be insane to jeopardize all that! It was political suicide!

Indeed, Boris Yeltsin did in a way die at that plenum—and was reborn as the most popular, trusted, and beloved political figure in the country.

Retaliation was swift and ruthless. Yeltsin was crucified by virtually every speaker who followed him, including Gorbachev and especially Ligachev. The one man who stood up for him was Yakovlev, but his call for leniency was not heard. Yeltsin was kicked off the Politburo and out of the Central Committee—which also "recommended" that he be "relieved" of his functions as Moscow's Party secretary. An extremely strong and healthy man, both physically and mentally, Yeltsin went to pieces as a result of the mass attack he was subjected to and wound up in the hospital with a minor heart condition. There he was pumped full of tranquilizers and literally dragged to a plenary session of the Moscow Party Committee. Befuddled and bewildered, Yeltsin had trouble understanding the stream of questions and invective showered on him; his answers sounded foolish, even stupid. Of course, the full protocol of those proceedings was published in the press. Yeltsin was pronounced "politically deceased," and appointed to the insignificant post of deputy chairman of the U.S.S.R. Construction Committee.

But while all of this was happening, something very unusual accompanied it. In the past, when a Party dignitary was "relieved" of his duties, the population reacted in one of two ways: with applause or with indifference. Either way, the people trusted their leaders to know who was right and who was wrong. Not this time. Suddenly Boris Yeltsin became a folk hero, a protector of the downtrodden. He most definitely was none of the above. But the unbelievable fact that he had had the courage to tweak the leadership's nose and say what a lot of average people felt—that made him a hero. And it could well be that Yeltsin became a different person because of what he suffered—and also because of the burden the people put on his shoulders when they made him their hero. Strange? Certainly. But stranger things have happened. Perhaps I should put that differently: Stranger things *did* happen.

I think it is fair to assume that Gorbachev wrote Yeltsin off. He had every reason to do so, for no one, repeat, no one had ever come back from that kind of political death. But this was a new ball game, so new that even its inventor Gorbachev did not fully understand the forces he had liberated. Even when he called for and pushed through the idea of national elections to the country's Supreme Soviet—the equivalent of Parliament—elections with multiple candidates on the ballot, with real choice, with no Party stamp of approval necessary, even then he could not have understood the real and full consequences of that decision.

For decades the voter turnout in the Soviet Union had always been over 99 percent, even though there had been only one name on the ballot. Initially that turnout had been a reflection of the population's trust in and support for their government, a kind of endorsement, rather than a vote. Over the years that huge turnout continued to reflect the trust of many but also the knowledge that if you did not vote, it would duly be noted in the registration books and might be interpreted as a lack of patriotism on your part—which could have dire consequences.

Then, in the Khrushchev and post-Khrushchev period, much of the vote was falsified; fewer and fewer people voted, but officers at the polling stations checked off their names on the lists and dropped the ballots in the boxes for them. By the time Gorbachev came around, cynicism and indifference had reached such a level that most people saw voting as a farce. Gorbachev wanted to change that. But he could hardly foresee that real elections would electrify all of Soviet society, that they would divide the country, that the Party and other groups euphemistically called "public organizations" would be forced to devise devious means by which to guarantee their representation in the nation's top legislative body.

When Yeltsin announced that he would run for a seat in Parliament, the establishment shrugged its collective shoulders. But as the "elect Yeltsin" campaign picked up steam, as it became more and more evident that running in his hometown of Sverdlovsk Yeltsin would be tough to beat, the establishment began to play dirty.

And the establishment was, first and foremost, Mikhail Sergeyevich Gorbachev. I certainly have no proof that he personally advised the running of the anti-Yeltsin campaign; I don't even know whether he gave his consent to it. But the fact is, he did nothing to stop it—although he easily could have. The smear campaign was not a novelty in the Soviet Union—countless "enemies of the people," scores of dissident writers, thinkers, activists had been subjected to the vilest slander and mudslinging. The novelty was the use of this in an election campaign. The real surprise, however, was that the campaign backfired completely and totally, bringing the undecided to cast their vote for Yeltsin.

By the time election day came around, all military men at

all bases all over the country had been *ordered* to vote against Yeltsin. The personnel of Soviet embassies, consulates, and diplomatic and trade missions had been "instructed" by their local Party secretary how to vote (due to rules and regulations, an embassy Party secretary was referred to as a "trade union secretary"). These heavy-handed tactics led to only three votes being cast against Yeltsin in the Soviet embassy in Washington, D.C. for instance, while in the Soviet Mission to the UN the number was even lower —one, to be precise. Boris Yeltsin's election was a triumph for the underdog, for the repressed and oppressed. Had Gorbachev been less self-centered and unforgiving, he would have seen it as a personal triumph, a triumph for the *perestroika* he had begun. It was, after all, proof positive that the people were indeed open to change and ready to move. But Gorbachev took it as a slap in the face.

At the first Congress of People's Deputies, now most remembered because of Andrei Sakharov's undaunted face-to-face confrontation with a largely hostile audience, Yeltsin took the floor and accused Gorbachev, but more specifically Ligachev, of applying the brakes to *perestroika*. Ligachev countered with a diatribe about how wonderfully well he had done when he was Party secretary of the Omsk *oblast,* and ended with a four-word clincher which, ever since, has become part of Russian lore: "Boris, you are wrong!"

But Boris was right. This Boris was a very different one from the man who had bitten off the heads of his subordinates when he was Party secretary of Moscow. This was a changed man who, indeed, had died a kind of death and then come back with a completely new view. And by the spring of 1990, he had become the number-one target on the hard-liners' hit list; it could even be said that open season had been declared on Yeltsin, for Gorbachev did nothing and said nothing to discourage the headhunters. And, as the Russian saying goes, silence means acquiescence.

I first met Yeltsin in early May of 1990, a few days prior to

the Russian Federation's parliamentary elections to the post
of chairman. I had been offered an interview with him and I
jumped at the chance to do a one-on-one with this Party
maverick. Not that I liked him or had great respect for him.
On the contrary, I was suspicious of his motives to the point
where I had been the first to call him the Huey Long of
Russia.

I can't say what kind of a man I expected to meet, but as I
recall how impressed I was by Yeltsin, I realize my expecta-
tions had been very different (and far more negative) than
what I encountered. The first thing that struck me when
Yeltsin came out of his office to greet me was how good he
looked. He was wearing a beautifully tailored navy blue suit
that set off his good color, blue eyes, and carefully trimmed
gray hair. There was a sense of robust health about him,
something very clean, no blurred edges; what you saw was
what you got—or at least it seemed so. He moved very
gracefully for a big, burly man, and his handshake was dry
and firm, though not to the point of "crushing" your hand
(a kind of macho password among Party officials).

While the final preparations were being made—we had
two cameras and a team of sound and lighting people—I
told Yeltsin that we had been given thirty minutes of air
time. I would try to keep the interview to precisely that
time, so as to exclude any editing of the tape. I also asked
him to keep his answers brief—that way I would be able to
ask a maximum number of questions.

Quite frankly, I was certain Yeltsin, a man with little television experience, would not be receptive to what I was asking. I was wrong. He was, in fact, exceptionally good. His
answers were concise, to the point, and he fielded the
toughest questions gracefully and forcefully. Here are just
two examples:

v.p.: Would you agree with the view that Boris Nikolayevich Yeltsin is a political speculator?

B.Y.: No. A man who takes risks—certainly. Because no politician can hope to achieve anything without risking something. But a speculator—absolutely not.

V.P.: People who worked with you in the past have told me you yell at your subordinates, bang your fists on the table. Would you call yourself a democrat?

B.Y.: No. You know where I come from, you know my background. There was nothing to make me democratic. I am trying to learn, and I hope the people around me help me to become more democratic. But because of my past, it will not be easy.

In that thirty-minute interview I managed to ask twenty questions and I was happy with nearly all of the answers. The two exceptions had to do with the Russian "patriotic" organization Pamyat. When I tried to get Yeltsin to clarify his position on anti-Semitism and the Pamyat people, he ducked the question and spoke about nationalism in general and its inevitability. When I tried to pin him down, he sidestepped the issue and criticized Gorbachev for not dealing properly with those issues.

After the interview, Yeltsin patted me on the back, gave me his famous cat smile—just the hint of a laugh in the corners of his mouth—and said, "I know what you wanted, but now is not the time for me to speak about it." Just what did that mean? Was he afraid he might lose part of the Russian vote if he made a strong statement about anti-Semitism? (A year and a half later, when Yeltsin participated in an ABC News "Town Hall" special with Peter Jennings and was asked about Pamyat, he again refused to take a stand. He gave a wishy-washy answer about Pamyat's supposedly having changed for the better. Meaning what, one could ask? Was it that Pamyat was now no longer anti-Semitic, no longer chauvinistic, no longer xenophobic? Yeltsin did not say.)

But with that notable exception, our interview was a gem —certainly the best he had done or has done to date. And that is precisely why it was not broadcast. The chairman of Gosteleradio prohibited its airing—and it was not an independent decision on his part. While I have no proof of this, I do not doubt the order came from the very top, that is, from President Gorbachev.

Not only was the interview not aired, but orders were given to destroy the tape—orders that were not obeyed. The tape was spirited away to Leningrad, where the local TV studio aired it. Since Leningrad TV can be seen in Moscow, as well as in many other regions of the country, the result was a double victory for Yeltsin: He had not only done very well in the interview, but had once again overcome his detractors. Not surprisingly, Yeltsin won the elections to the chairmanship of the Russian Federation's Parliament.

No sooner had Yeltsin been elected, he made it absolutely clear that his priority was Russia—her interests, here and now as well as in the future. Suddenly Russia, which had really never had a clear identity, often being confused by many with the Soviet Union, began to emerge as a separate entity with a highly visible leader. Prior to that, in most people's minds the equation was Gorbachev = the U.S.S.R. (Russia). Now it was Yeltsin = Russia; Gorbachev = ?

Representing Russia and with Russia fully behind him, Yeltsin was a power, a fact that both frightened and angered the conservatives. That fright and anger turned to panic and fury when Yeltsin called for, and conducted, a poll in Russia on the subject of whether or not Russia should have a president. The answer was a resounding Yes!—an answer that galvanized the anti-Yeltsin forces into action. As they saw it, there was only one way to deal with the situation and that was to oust Yeltsin from his post of chairman, thereby making his presidential bid look very weak. They decided that the best time and place to challenge Yeltsin would be during Russian Parliament's Congress in March 1991.

Rumors about this forthcoming confrontation began to circulate almost immediately. The pro-democracy forces called for a mass meeting on Manezh Square, opposite the Kremlin, on the Congress's opening day. The anti-Yeltsin forces countered with ugly rumors about plans on the part of the "democrats" to storm the Kremlin and take power. Supposedly the mass meeting was only a cover-up for what would happen: A special team of mountain climbers, each climber armed with a hook and ropes, would scale the Kremlin walls, take out the guards, and then the mad crowd would rush in and physically destroy whatever political opponents Yeltsin had in the Russian Parliament. Reacting to that "threat," some twenty deputies appealed to the government for protection, saying they feared for their lives.

Now, all of this was absolute hogwash, the most unbelievable piece of disinformation imaginable. Nevertheless, Gorbachev used it. He prohibited the mass rally and he allowed the military to bring tanks and armored vehicles into Moscow.

Since the arrest of KGB chief Beria in 1953, when tanks were ordered into Moscow by Khrushchev just in case the KGB tried to save its boss, the streets had never been occupied by military vehicles and men. The measure was aimed at scaring the population away from the Kremlin, but it boomeranged: Hundreds and then thousands came to Manezh Square, showing complete disregard for Gorbachev's orders. Once again, Yeltsin exploited the situation perfectly. He refused to open the Congress. Instead, he came out of the Kremlin to address the vast crowd. To thunderous applause and roars of approval he said that he would not be daunted by the military, that the Congress would not go into session until every tank and armored car left the city, every soldier and officer had returned to his quarters.

The authorities had no choice but to back down. On the following morning not a trace of the military could be found in the city. Yeltsin had won again. And even though he was

furiously attacked by his opponents in the Russian Parliament, even though several of the deputies called for his
resignation, they were fighting for a lost cause.

Yeltsin had faced down the government, and his stature
was even greater.

By the same token, Gorbachev's stature was again diminished. The hard-liners who had always had their doubts
about Gorbachev and who had always accused him of being
"soft," and the powerful clan of *oblast* (regional) Party secretaries, especially those who formed the backbone of the
Russian Communist Party, headed by Ivan Polozkov, decided that the only way to really change things was to rid
themselves of Gorbachev. The Party structures were still all
there; they had not been dismantled. With Gorbachev out
of Party office, with a hard-liner as general secretary, Gorbachev the president could be controlled and the whole process of *perestroika* reversed.

That was the sense of a speech delivered by Polozkov in
early February, when he stated that "we all now realize that
perestroika, formulated in 1985 and started by the Party and
the people as the renewal of socialism, a more dynamic and
fuller application of socialism's potential for economic, cultural, and democratic growth, for improving the living standard of the people, has not happened."

Addressing an assembly of Party members, priests, and
descendents of Russian noblemen in early March, Polozkov
made an even stronger statement:

". . . The destructive anti-government and anti-national
forces, comprised by many who formerly constituted the
ideological elite and who participated in the country's
breakdown during the so-called period of stagnation, who in
those times were rewarded with huge fortunes and scientific
degrees and who now have changed their clothing and who
dress up as radical democrats, they have seized the mass
media, they are actively in the process of transforming a
great power into a raw material appendage of transnational

corporations. Pluralism has quickly changed to radical democratic dictatorship, while emulation of American democracy has become a means of destroying the U.S.S.R.'s integrity with the aim of then dividing Russia into fiefdoms, sovereign republics, federal districts, and free economic zones."

The anti-Gorbachev onslaught was planned for the April 1991 plenum of the Central Committee. Gorbachev had been under fire before, but for those of us—journalists and others—who had followed the years of *perestroika* with a watchful eye, this time things really looked bad: Gorbachev had backed away from his liberal supporters in October of 1990 to join the right wing, but now that very same right wing was refusing to carry him any longer. He was alone and it was hard to see who could possibly save him. It could only be someone who needed Gorbachev . . . and that person, ironically, was Yeltsin. It was the most logical thing. Neither of them was strong enough to overcome the other, but together there was virtually nothing they could not do. By April Yeltsin had realized it was far better to have a strong Gorbachev in office both as president of the U.S.S.R. and general secretary of the Communist Party of the Soviet Union, than to have him as a weakened president with a hard-liner running the Party.

I would not be surprised to learn that Yeltsin had secretly contacted Gorbachev and had proposed a pact. Both men were certainly aware of what was being planned and both had to realize they needed each other. I would also not be surprised to learn that Yeltsin had contacted the presidents of the nine Union republics that had in principle agreed to be the signatories to a Union treaty.

Whether or not these clandestine contacts were made remains to be seen, but we do know that on April 23, 1991, just *two days* before the opening of the Central Committee plenum where Gorbachev was to be handed his head, nine presidents and Gorbachev (this giving birth to the formula,

Nine Plus One) signed their "Common Statement on Immediate Measures to Stabilize the Country and Overcome the Crisis." The Common Statement sent a powerful three-pronged message to the country:

- Gorbachev and Yeltsin have joined forces.
- The republics will now enjoy much greater independence.
- The Union treaty will leave the central government with very little authority.

I believe it was then that the idea of a coup was first seriously considered, for a coup was the only way of destroying the Nine Plus One alliance which, if allowed to progress, would undeniably destroy the old power structure.

Gorbachev was alive. My initial belief of Monday morning that he had been killed, that the official announcement of his "illness" would escalate to "serious condition" and culminate in a somber announcement of the president's death due to cardiovascular failure or some massive hemorrhage, turned out to be wrong. The leaders of the coup needed Gorbachev; they could not afford to kill him. I have often thought about the reasons why President Gorbachev refused to put his name to the State of Emergency decree, why he refused to sign it. He has answered that question, saying he was completely against the idea, that he wanted to put it before the Supreme Soviet, let the people's representatives in office, the deputies, make that decision. While I do not doubt Gorbachev's honesty in that matter, I cannot help but think that he had to know his very life depended on that signature. Had he signed the decree, he could very conveniently "pass away": The signature legitimized the process, its authenticity could easily be proven. As long as he did not sign, he had a chance.

At noon on the twenty-first, President Yeltsin's press secretary, Pavel Voshchanov, had officially announced that the leadership of the Russian government had reached an agreement with KGB head Kryuchkov to fly together to Gorbachev's Black Sea residence in the Crimea. It was then and only then that the Central Committee of the Communist Party of the Soviet Union suddenly showed its face: Gorbachev's deputy, Vladimir Ivashko, called on Vice President Yanayev and "demanded" a meeting with the general secretary. Many people have had harsh things to say about the Central Committee's members and top Party officials. I support those statements. If I had to select just one word to describe the basic trait characterizing all of them, that word would be hypocrisy. Ivashko's sudden "demand" was a stunning example of hypocrisy.

The Central Committee had squarely backed the coup. The mass media during those three days had been tightly controlled by one of the top Politburo members, a certain Mr. Dzasokhov. The coup was not simply backed by the Central Committee, it was inspired by the Committee's most hard-line members. The eight coupsters who made up the Emergency Committee were all members of the Central Committee. As soon as the state of emergency was announced, the Party dropped its general secretary like a hot potato. It had vanished but now it was back, indignantly demanding access to its leader.

Soon after Voshchanov's announcement, I learned from my own sources that Kryuchkov had deliberately misled Yeltsin and the Russian government. He had promised to fly with a Yeltsin delegation, but instead he joined up with Defense Minister Yazov and a few other members of the Emergency Committee, slipped out of Moscow, and boarded a plane that took off in what was first called "an unknown direction." There was even a rumor that these men had asked for, and received, political asylum in North Korea.

There were all kinds of contradictory reports, including one circulated by Agence France Press that the entire Emergency Committee had been arrested before they could board a plane at Vnukovo airport and escape. In fact, at four in the afternoon Russian Vice President Rutskoy, together with Russian Prime Minister Silayev, several other officials, and a platoon of security, arrived at Vnukovo where they were informed that several of the coupsters had departed only a few minutes earlier, that they were headed toward the Crimea and that they had commandeered two large passenger jets—one for themselves and one for Gorbachev. Even that information turned out to be somewhat inaccurate.

Kryuchkov, Yazov, Lukyanov, and others boarded an IL-62 passenger jet at 2:18 P.M. and landed at an airport not far from Gorbachev's summer residence in Phoros at 4:08 P.M. A second plane left Vnukovo at twenty minutes to three—this was a TU-134 passenger jet—and landed at the same place at 4:30 P.M. Prime Minister Silayev, Vice President Rutskoy, Vadim Bakatin, and ten other officials along with security took off from Vnukovo Airport on a TU-134 at eight minutes to five. At some point between 7:30 P.M. and 8:00 P.M., they were received by Gorbachev, who had left Lukyanov, Kyruchkov, Yazov, and company to cool their heels, refusing even to acknowledge their presence.

Ah, Mikhail Sergeyevich, I thought to myself, how long it took you to understand who were your friends and who were your enemies, how tragically long. I wondered if he had forgotten the day and time when, in October 1987, angered at Yeltsin's harsh words concerning how slow progress had been, he had turned on him and said: "I will not allow you into politics, Boris." Yes, he had actually said those words, as if he had the power, like a tsar of sorts, to either open or close the door to whoever might wish to become actively involved in the political process.

I wondered if he recalled how he had dropped his staunchest supporters. How, one by one, he had let them go, throwing them like a bone to the ravenous pack of right-wing hounds that bayed at his heels. First Bakatin, then Shevardnadze, then Shatalin, Petrakov, even Yakovlev.

I tried to imagine what kind of torture he had experienced when people he had intimately trusted betrayed him—Boldin, Yazov, Kryuchkov, his personal bodyguard Medvedev, the head of the Secret Service, Plekhanov. And what about Yanayev, the man he rammed through Parliament, the man he publicly referred to as "an active participant in *perestroika*" whom "he trusted unconditionally"? Later Gorbachev would admit this would always haunt him—and well it should, to his very grave. It was because of his misplaced trust that we had been pushed to the edge of the abyss. . . .

Ugly rumors had begun to circulate around Moscow on that last day of the coup, rumors that Gorbachev was involved in the plot, had known about it from day one, that once again in his inimitable way he had survived by allowing the events to play themselves out before committing himself. I did not believe that. It was enough to see his face as he emerged from the plane that brought him back from the Crimea in the early morning hours of August 22 to understand that he had not been part of the coup. But even then, safe and sound, home free, he blundered again: Instead of going directly to the White House to thank the people who had saved his life, instead of going there to publicly shake Yeltsin's hand, Gorbachev went home.

I thought of the three days and nights he had spent,

locked away from the rest of the world, and this biblical passage came to mind:

"And he was three days without sight . . . Immediately there fell from his eyes something like scales, and he reached his sight at once . . ." (Acts 9).

I asked myself what would have happened had Gorbachev supported Yeltsin from the outset? Had he stood by his principles and the men who supported them? Had he acted decisively and followed the advice of people like Andrei Sakharov? Had he agreed to grant the republics independence and had offered them the same kind of Union treaty then—in 1987–88—as he was forced to do in 1991?

In so many respects Gorbachev had done everything too late. Measures that would have been wildly successful a year or two earlier were bypassed by events by the time he adopted them. Finally, that was why he, President Mikhail Sergeyevich Gorbachev, was more to blame than anyone else for the coup. . . .

Flashback: The Calm Before the Storm

The six years of Gorbachev's *perestroika* had been an unending struggle of one group to preserve the status quo and of another to change it. Not a day had passed without some phase of that struggle being fought. Sometimes it was a brief skirmish, sometimes a bloody battle. One of the first and bloodiest raged around whether or not to abolish Article VI of the Soviet constitution, which enshrined the Communist Party of the Soviet Union as the country's "leading force."

The conservatives were still poorly organized in the early days. Gorbachev was inclined to be on the liberal side, so after much to-ing and fro-ing Article VI was voted out of the constitution by the Congress of People's Deputies of the U.S.S.R. and thus ceased to exist.

The Party, however, did not. Even though it was no longer the country's officially recognized supreme arbiter and decision maker, the Communist Party continued to call the shots. Anything and everything of any importance had to go through the Politburo. The vast network of Party organizations, headed by some forty thousand full-time Party secretaries, continued to hold the country in its spider web. What soon became apparent was that as long as the Party continued to have a presence in the workplace, in the armed forces, in the police and the KGB, in short, everywhere, Article VI continued to exist, if not in letter, then certainly in spirit.

Proponents of real change began to call for phasing out the Party's influence—they called it departization. Let the Party have its headquarters, they said. Let Party members have meetings, if that is their desire, but let that all be outside the workplace. As for the armed forces, the police, and the KGB, there should be no room for party activities in those organizations.

That view was anathema to the Party leadership, Gorbachev included, for quite obvious reasons: Without that presence, the Party could no longer hope to control everyday decisions; it would lose the omnipresence that made it so powerful.

By the time Boris Yeltsin was elected president of Russia in June of 1991, nothing had really changed at all. The liberals were, as the conservatives put it, still yapping about departization, but the Party structure was, if anything, even stronger than before, especially in the armed forces, where with Gorbachev's blessing an All-Armed Forces Party Committee had been created.

Imagine, then, the reaction when Boris Yeltsin issued a presidential decree—one of his first—outlawing Party presence in the workplace. Of course, this theoretically applied to *all* political parties, but for practical purposes the decree was aimed only at the Communist Party.

The ensuing outcry was a combination of rage and fear. Suddenly all the hard-liners became great upholders of democratic process and demanded that the Constitutional Committee determine whether or not Yeltsin's decree violated the law of the land. They decried this act which "infringed on the rights of rank-and-file Party members." They called on all "true democrats" to come to the defense of Soviet society, to prevent its becoming an ochlocracy.

The loudest cry of all appeared in the July 23 issue of *Sovetskaya Rossiya,* the same paper that had published Nina Andreyeva's "letter" some four years earlier. This time it was not a letter, but rather an appeal addressed to "The People" by its twelve signatories. It opened in apocalyptic tones:

"Dear Russians! Citizens of the U.S.S.R! A terrible and unheard of blight is upon us. . . . Our Motherland, our country, our great state . . . are dying, disintegrating, sinking into darkness and oblivion." The entire appeal continued in the same vein, drawing the most dire picture of the country's present and of what horrible suffering awaited it . . . if the people did not rise up and act.

The "horror" that the signatories had in mind was, of course, Yeltsin's departization plan—as was soon evidenced when the liberal weekly *Ogonyok* magazine interviewed Gennadi Dzyuganov, a Politburo member of the Russian Communist Party and certainly one of its most intelligent members, who commented:

"Do you think one can be indifferent to the way they are destroying our State? Do you consider it normal when Boris Nikolayevich [Yeltsin], instead of taking a hard look at society's real problems, decides to rid plants and enterprises of Party committees? I was shocked by that decree. . . . Russians have an old history of working together, collectively.

But now a blow has been delivered at a time when 30 percent of the harvest may be lost, which in turn will mean even less food for the northern areas of the country, where the situation is fraught with tension and the danger of exploding. Nor should one forget that most collective farm chairmen are members of the Communist Party. Who knows what that decree could lead to in a country crammed with nuclear and chemical weapons, what kinds of dangers are inherent in the increasingly tense situation? . . . As for the Communist Party, it has nothing to be ashamed of, nothing to repent about, except for having allowed power to be taken away and passed on to a bunch of parliamentarians. . . ."

After the publication of the Yeltsin decree, it finally and beyond question of a doubt became evident that the Party stalwarts had indeed come out of the trenches. They had really not done that six months earlier, when Gorbachev had called on them to do so. But now, having fully realized how far things had gone and knowing that if things went any further the Party would have to accept defeat, they decided to strike back with every piece of weaponry at their disposal. The time and place were carefully selected: Moscow, July 25, 1991, the plenary meeting of the Central Committee.

In a way, the atmosphere was very much like that of the days preceding the April Central Committee plenum when the *oblast* secretaries plotted to knock Gorbachev out of the box and replace him with one of their own. The plot fell through thanks to Boris Yeltsin and eight other republic presidents who teamed up with Gorbachev for the Nine Plus One declaration. But now was a different time. Now it was do or die—and the Party elite were certainly not inclined to give up the ghost.

The plenum opened as scheduled on July 25, and General Secretary Gorbachev delivered what had to be one of the strongest, most radical, most ground-breaking speeches in his entire career. For the first time in the history of Central Committee gatherings the general secretary did not once reiterate his faith in Marxism-Leninism. He gave but the most passing mention of Communism's promises and made statements for which anyone in the Soviet Union would have been summarily shot during the Stalin period, jailed and sent out to the gulag under Khrushchev and Brezhnev, committed to an insane asylum under Andropov, and kicked out of the Party under Gorbachev himself. To wit:

"In past times the Party swore by one thing only, Marxism-Leninism, never mind that it distorted the teaching beyond recognition, thereby serving its pragmatic aims and finally transforming Marxism into a kind of canonic prayer book. The time has come to enrich our outlook with the product of international socialist and democratic thought.

"A Party member has the right to freely express his views, to be an atheist or to practice a religion; he is free to actively work in a Party organization or to support the Party in whatever other way he sees fit.

"Our Party undisputably bears the responsibility for not having blocked despotism, for having allowed itself to be used as an instrument of totalitarianism."

As I listened, I found myself doubting my ears. Was this really Gorbachev, or had someone slipped in a perfect lookalike? The general secretary was in effect breaking away from some of the Party's most basic tenets formulated by none other than Vladimir Lenin himself. This was heresy; this was like walking naked into a den full of hungry jackals.

Amazing? My God, yes! But not even mildly surprising compared to the incredible fact that the jackals *all applauded, and then took the floor to express their regrets at having attacked Gorbachev in the past!* All was serenity and forgiveness, the Party was being reborn a gentler and kinder type of animal.

I could not believe it. Neither could most of my friends. But what was the motive for this change of heart? There were two basic views on that. One was that, faced with Yeltsin's departization decree and the threat it carried, the Party leadership had called off the anti-Gorbachev onslaught; instead, all efforts were to be directed at mending the rifts, consolidating the ranks, and rebuilding—be it only for a relatively short period of time—the invincible monolith that had been the Party in the past.

The second view—which I tend to give more credit to—is that by the time the plenum assembled, the Central Committee's most adamant opponents of change had decided that Gorbachev's ouster as general secretary and his replacement by a hard-liner was not going to be enough to turn the tide. As long as the Nine Plus One equation continued to exist, the change was unstoppable. These people understood that the Nine Plus One combination was really much more like "1 + 1 + 8," the first "one" being not Gorbachev (he was the second), but Boris Yeltsin. Take out Yeltsin, and Gorbachev would be isolated and not difficult to deal with: The other eight would immediately crumble into several separate and therefore easy to handle units.

This, I believe, is when a coup was first seriously considered as the only option. They had tried to stop Yeltsin on more than one occasion. Each time they had failed, and after every failure Yeltsin came back stronger than before. Gorbachev was, in their opinion, a much easier target, and not the least reason for that was the population's dislike for him and for the reforms he symbolized. Getting rid of Gorbachev was really not a problem. Getting rid of Yeltsin was. In my opinion, the real thrust of the coup was aimed at Yeltsin—and the plotters hoped that Gorbachev with his "Yeltsin allergy" would not interfere. Having made that decision, the Party bosses called off their dogs and made a show of solidarity with the general secretary.

And thus the nation was treated to a lullaby. In a way it made me think of the summer of 1990, when five days a week on the morning show Soviet State Television featured a healer who told two hundred million people to close their eyes, relax, and take heart in his incantation: "All is well, don't worry, be happy . . ."

And sure enough, many people believed it.

It was near midnight of August 21. Without waiting to be invited, many of our friends had come to our home to celebrate—for some reason we were picked as the center to gravitate toward. We were all in a state hard to describe. Laughter came as easily as tears. Food was plentiful (as had always been the case, if one could afford the prices of the free farmers' market), and so was vodka. We were all on a high—not really because of the alcohol we had consumed, but because of the sense of victory, the wonderful victory we had snatched from the very jaws of defeat.

I had gone upstairs for a minute to watch the late-night news—there was really nothing on it that I did not know—and now had come out on the stairs. As I looked down at my friends, people I loved dearly, as I felt a wave of joy sweep over me at the thought that now we were all safe, that we had broken into the sunlight after endless years of darkness, I found myself thinking: "Thank you, Mikhail Sergeyevich." Because just as surely as he was to blame for the coup, so was he the reason why the coup failed.

As I have pointed out, the men who led the coup had everything going for them: the armed forces, the KGB, the Party, the police. But most importantly of all, they had precedent going for them. They had history going for them; they had the absolute and irrefutable knowledge that never ever had the Soviet people opposed authority. Just as *these men* had been brought up to fear and to obey, just as *these men* had been taught that nothing could stand up to the Party machine, just as *these men* would not have dreamed of challenging the powers that be, neither could they imagine anyone else's doing that.

And they were absolutely right. Perhaps a few dissidents had broken with tradition, but they were the exception to the rule, not really a force to be reckoned with. I repeat, these men were absolutely right—but they were trapped in a time that had ended five years earlier. Always out of touch with the people, this elite—the privileged bureaucracy, the Party-military-KGB-government machine—never really believed in *perestroika,* never really accepted the very Marxist proposition that *if you could change the human condition, then you could change what was considered the human character.* Gorbachev had changed the conditions—and the people had changed. Not all of them, as witnessed by how many looked the other way, refused to become involved when the coup occurred, but a sufficient number to make the coup fail. So in a most fascinating and seemingly contradictory way, Gorbachev was responsible for both the coup and for its failure, for the tragedy and the triumph, for bringing us all to the edge of the abyss and for helping us span the chasm.

I quietly left the apartment, slipping out unnoticed, and walked up my street, then turned left on Shchukin Street to the Ring road, right, and all the way to the underpass where three young men had died fighting for freedom. The gutted carcasses of trolleys stood there, where they had taken the first onslaught of armored cars. People stood holding candles, some quietly weeping, others celebrating.

From the top of the underpass I could see the white-blue-red flag of Russia, now the official flag, flying atop the White House. Back in the late seventeenth century, when Peter the Great visited Holland, he was very taken with the Dutch flag: three broad horizontal stripes, red on top, then white, finally sky blue. Tsar Peter, a man who had never cared about convention, decided then and there what would be Russia's flag: the Dutch flag slightly jumbled; three broad horizontal stripes, white-blue-red.

I thought of that, looking at the flag from afar, the flag waving in the rays of the spotlights that were trained on it, and I asked myself: Would Russia, that wonderful country blessed with such a great people, a country that had been jumbled for so long, would it now finally come together?

The Aftermath

We are in the process of witnessing the aftershocks of the coup. In a peculiar way, it led to premature birth.

I once wrote that the process of *perestroika* was akin to the birth of a nation—with all the pain and blood that birth involves. A painful process, to be sure, especially when applying to nearly three hundred million people of different nationalities, cultures, heritages, creeds, and languages. And yet a natural process, an inevitable process.

The coup changed all that. Unnatural as it was—as any coup cannot but be—it has created a host of unforeseen problems, while compounding others. Instead of due process there is chaos. Passions have replaced common sense and reason. The heady dreams of independence have clouded the minds of millions. In the murky waters that boil through the crumbling dam, politicians hope to catch the big one.

Playing to populist instincts and chauvinistic prejudices, politicians rupture the ties that have held this calico-quilt of a country together for centuries. The Ukraine calls for the creation of its own armed forces, an expense it can hardly afford, and looks nervously over its shoulder at a Russia that desires to take back the Crimean peninsula which a magnanimous Khrushchev "gave" to the Ukraine when nobody dreamed of the country's future dismemberment. Moldavia refuses to have even an economic agreement with whatever is left of what was once the U.S.S.R., wishing to merge with Romania, one of the world's poorest—and least democratic—countries. Georgia stands proudly independent, headed by a former dissident who publicly demonstrated his cowardice when he recanted on national television in Brezhnev's times and now refuses to grant independence to any of the ethnic minorities in the country he leads. Armenia and Azerbaijan glare at each other and shed each other's blood in what seems to be a dead-end struggle over territory both lay claims to. The Baltic States, now officially independent, adopt laws that would be called repressive and even fascistic; they face an uncertain economic future, depending as they do on Russia's natural resources for energy and raw material. As for the republics of Soviet Central Asia . . . only in one of them, Kirghizia, was there any opposition to the coup. In the others—Uzbekistan, Turkmenistan, Tadzhikistan—where the Communist Party leadership had never really been challenged, where former Communist Party leaders had quietly moved into the presidencies, the coup was greeted with delight—and action. All pro-*perestroika* newspapers were shut down, censorship was reintroduced, Gorbachev's pictures were quickly removed from office walls. After the failure of the coup and Yeltsin's decree curtailing the activities of the Communist Party, the presidents of those republics—again, with the exception of Kirghizia—immediately announced the breakaway of their local Communist parties from the Communist Party of the Soviet Union. What that really meant was that Yeltsin's decree would not affect them, since the Uzbek or the Tadzhik Communist Party was no longer a structural part of the banned Communist Party of the Soviet Union. Thus the old structures remained intact and the old players continued to control the game. But a new element was added: the element of Muslim fundamentalism. Feeling more and more cut off from the radical mainstream of Russia and the other European republics, the republics of Central Asia have begun to take refuge in the fundamental teachings of Islam. The consequences of these changes are impossible to predict.

Kazakhstan, that huge land mass, second only to Russia in size, but tiny and predominantly Russian in population, immensely wealthy in mineral resources and quasi-feudal in development and living standards, led by powerful and brilliant President Nazarbayev, remains one of the biggest question marks: Which way will it ultimately go?

Byelorussia, ravaged by the aftermath of Chernobyl, a land that never had independence or statehood, but that is now waking up to the reality of that possibility—its awakening, as is often the case, being accompanied by a virulent nationalism, translated in this case into anti-Semitism—is another unpredictable factor in the general equation.

And finally there is Russia. Even without any of the former republics, it is the largest land mass in the world, probably the richest country in the world in natural resources—a nation that boasts a proud heritage of scientists and writers, composers and painters, statesmen and athletes, a highly educated nation. Yet it is a nation mired in poverty, thrashing about in the agony of drawing its first fresh breath, unhappy with its past and unsure of its future, the possible easy prey of some local fascist type. An example of this is Vladimir Zhirinovsky, a man who has repeatedly called on Russians to rise up against ''kikes and commies, American imperialists and slant-eyed Japs,'' a man who could, if the situation continues to deteriorate in Russia, be democratically elected to office—as Hitler was in Germany.

All these are possibilities. For every bad scenario, there is a good one. Is the glass half full or half empty? That really depends on the dynamics: Is it in the process of being emptied or of being filled?

The convulsions and hardships notwithstanding, there are reasons to believe the glass is being filled. My hope lies with Russia. That is where history will be made. That, in my opinion, is where one can look to with hope. The people of Russia have gone through nearly seven and a half decades of the most harrowing social experiment ever conducted and they have come out of it alive. They have come out of it wiser, more compassionate, more spiritual—I use that word in its broadest sense—than most nations on Earth.

It will take time. It is very hard and will get harder. This winter of 1991–1992 could well be a tragic time, especially if the people of Russia conclude that the Western world is indifferent to their sufferings. But even then, they will prevail. In the words of William Gladstone:

"You cannot fight against the future. Time is on our side."

About the Author

VLADIMIR POZNER is the author of *Parting with Illusions* and co-host of the *Pozner & Donahue* television show. On April 15, 1991, he resigned from Soviet State Television, protesting the ban on any criticism of Gorbachev.